BC.

POPE JOHN PAUL II
ON
INCULTURATION

Theory and Practice

With love and appreciation
from the Author
Audoidem
Jan 17, 1997

S. Iniobong Udoidem

University Press of America, Inc.
Lanham • New York • London

Copyright © 1996 by
University Press of America,® Inc.
4720 Boston Way
Lanham, Maryland 20706

3 Henrietta Street
London, WC2E 8LU England

Library of Congress Cataloging-in-Publication Data

Udoidem, S. Inoibong.
Pope John Paul II on inculturation : theory and practice / S. Iniobong
Udoidem.
p.   cm.
Includes bibliographical references and index.
1. Christianity and culture--History--20th century. 2. Catholic
Church--Doctrines--History--20th century. 3. John Paul II, Pope,
1920--Contributions in doctrine of inculturation.   I. Title.
BR115.C8U36   1996   261'.08'822--dc20   96-33331 CIP

ISBN 0-7618-0502-8 (cloth: alk: ppr.)

Dedicated to:

**The Sacred Heart of Jesus the
Heart of Love
and
His Holiness Pope John Paul II on
the Occasion of the Golden Jubilee of
his Priestly Ordination (November 1, 1996).**

CONTENTS

FOREWORD I

One of the fascinating things about Pope John Paul II is that he is a man with deep faith and of personal conviction. He lives and believes what he teaches and teaches what he believes with so much passion and conviction that one cannot but listen to what he has to say. This I would say is the secret of his endearment: the youths of the world are charmed by his person, the older generation find in his teachings, a hope for the future, even his critics find him irresistible.

Books have been written on Pope John Paul II, but no where, to my knowledge has the unity of his thought and teaching been thematized with such lucidity and clarity as has been achieved by the book, *Pope John Paul II on Inculturation: Theory and Practice* by Rev. Fr. S. Iniobong Udoidem.

Evangelization is the core and the soul of the Church's mission. Pope John Paul II, in his New Era of Evangelization program has proposed inculturation as "the way" of the new evangelization. He has made it the *lait motif*, a recurring theme in his various pastoral journeys throughout the world's continents. The author's incisive insight, has ably captured the Pope's vision of the transcendental nature of the Goodnews vis - a-vis particular cultures. I must admit, that while the Holy Father has shown the way, Fr. Udoidem's book has explained the "what" and the "how" of inculturation.

One of philosophy's responsibility to other disciplines, is the clarification and setting of boundaries of understanding. It is in the light of this responsibility that Father Udoidem's book, which serves as both a philosophical analysis and a theological reflection on the concept of inculturation, has made a monumental contribution both in the clarification effort and in the highlighting of the teaching of the church on the subject. His work has provided a new philosophical insight into the nature and relevance of inculturation as a paradigm for the new era of evangelization. It is indeed an epoch breaking insight on the new evangelization.

The text has painstakingly traced inculturation to originative events, such as creation and incarnation, and shows how inculturation is effected in the divine as well as the human socio-dynamics. Thus one can say, that, with a mind of a wayward intellectual genius, Father Udoidem has managed to treat a difficult and complex subject in such a way that it does not only make for easy reading but appeals to all Christians as a way of life.

Inculturation is not easy, but it is a necessary task that must be done with all the urgency which the Pope's challenge of the New Era of Evangelization demands. For the achievement of our collective purpose as a church, it is here recommended that all pastoral agents and ministers of the Word, should read this new book studiously and have it as a guide for their understanding of the mind of the *Magisterium* on the subject. All Departments of

Philosophy, Centers for Cultural Studies, Seminaries and Theological institutions should have the book in their libraries. Indeed, it is a book that all Christians should have and read for the understanding of their vocation as Christians.

Most Rev. Alexius O. Makozi
Bishop of Port Harcourt - Nigeria.
Member, Pontifical Council "Cor Unum."

FOREWORD II

I am pleased to recommend and applaud *Pope John Paul II on Inculturation: Theory and Practice* by the Reverend Sylvanus Udoidem, a priest from Nigeria presently serving faithfully and effectively as a parish priest in the Diocese of Charleston. Just the circumstances of Father Udoidem's major education here in the United States and his ministry among us serve to make his insights into the very sensitive and serious phenomenon of inculturation valuable, informed, practical. He knows the field for having studied, lived it and embraced it, he appreciates that inculturation is indeed an incarnation, the incarnation of the Christian life and the Christian message into a particular culture to animate it, direct it so as to bring out a new creation.

May Father Udoidem's efforts find reward in bringing out new creation in our third millennium efforts of evangelization.

Most Rev. David B. Thompson
Bishop of Charleston
U.S.A.

ACKNOWLEDGMENTS

Writing an acknowledgment of a people and sources that have affected one's project is an uneasy task. Uneasy, not because one cannot remember the persons, times and circumstances but because, the persons and events are so numerous that it would be impossible to end the list without omitting some names and sources. I hope, therefore, that my benefactors would pardon me if I end the list before reaching their names. Their names are written boldly in my heart and I remember and cherish their contribution dearly.

I am grateful to His Holiness, Pope John Paul II for his boldness of thought and insights on Inculturation. His ideas have served as the fountain head upon which my thoughts in this text have been organized.

His Lordship, Rt. Rev. Joseph E. Ekuwem, D.D., the Bishop of Uyo, my home diocese deserves special thanks. His interest in excellence and in having the best for Uyo diocese led to his encouragement of my research projects. His permission that I serve in Port Harcourt diocese is a testimony to his missionary and Macedonian concerns.

His Lordship, Most Rev. Alexius O Makozi, D.D., the Bishop of Port Harcourt, in whose diocese I have served for the past ten years has been a wonderful inspiration to me. This project would not have been possible without his encouragement. He was the first to read the proposal, after which he encouraged me to take a Sabbatical Leave from my responsibilities as Chaplain and Lecturer, to carry out the research. When the research was completed he was there to write the *Foreword*.

I wish to thank Professor Timi Briggs, the former Acting Vice Chancellor and Professor Theo Vincent the current Vice Chancellor, of the University of Port Harcourt, for granting me the Sabbatical Leave for the purpose of carrying out this research.

I am thankful to the Center for Philosophy of Religion, University of Notre Dame, for awarding me the Fellowship that provided the financial guarantee for the research and publication of this text.

Professor Jude Dougherty, Dean of the School of Philosophy, Catholic University of America deserves special mention. He is always there as a moral booster for my academic endeavors. I wish to thank Professor George F. Mclean, Secretary, Council for Research in Values and Philosophy, Washington DC., for making the resources at the Council available to me. Here, I would like to thank the Paulist Press, for the permission to reprint Peter Schineller's diagram from Peter Schineller, *A Hand Book on Inculturation*, (New York: Paulist Press, 1990). I must also acknowledge here, that all biblical citations in the text are from the Saint Joseph edition of the New Catholic Holy Bible, (New York: Catholic Book Publications, 1963).

To my special friends in the United States of America, I say thank you for your friendship and support. Special thanks to His Lordship, Most Rev. David Thompson, D.D., J.C.L, the Bishop of Charleston, who not only welcomed me in his diocese but showed so much interest in my project to the point of accepting to write a *Foreword* for the text. Many thanks also to Most Rev. John M. D'Arcy, D.D., of the diocese of Fort Wayne - South Bend, for providing accommodation for me during my residency at the University of Notre Dame.

The Rev. Msgr. Joseph Roth, the Staff, Parishioners

Acknowledgements

and students of St. Andrew's Church and School, Myrtle Beach, were absolutely fabulous. I thank them for their love and friendliness. My appreciation also goes to Fr. Leonard Chrobot, professor of Sociology at the University of Notre Dame and his parishioners at St. Hedwig, South Bend. These friends deserve special mention for their support: Rev Fr. Eugene Leonard, Stephen and Alice Kiersynowski, Mary and Irv Marlar, Dr. Chris and Derby Borst, Wayne and Terry Wieble, Salvotore Amendola, John and Carthy Cummings, Mr. Patrick Ikart, and Mrs Bernadette Labruce who proof-read the introductory section of the text.

Many thanks to my colleagues in the Department of Philosophy, the students and members of the Chapel of the Annunciation Chaplaincy, University of Port Harcourt, the Regina Coeli Old Boys Association, Port Harcourt Branch, and Mboho Mkparawa Ibibio National Council, and the Nigerian Community in Horry County, South Carolina, for their encouragement and support.

Finally, to the members of my family and friends, I say, thank you and may God bless you for your fidelity and love.

Like all human productions, this text may not be without limitations, omissions and even mistakes. I plead, therefore, with all humility that I be held excused, for, I too, I am human.

Rev. Fr. S. Iniobong Udoidem, P.hD
Department of Philosophy and Religious Studies
University of Port Harcourt
Port Harcourt - Nigeria

INTRODUCTION

It is sometimes amazing if not surprising how books come to be written. The seminal ideas of this book began in January of 1995, when Rev Fr. Justin Ukpong, the Editor of the *Journal of Inculturation*, at the Catholic Institute of West Africa, Port Harcourt, asked me to do an article on the "Philosophy of Inculturation" for his Journal. I immediately commenced reading on the subject. But, the more I read, the more I discovered that very few writers on inculturation really understood the mind of the official Church on the subject. It was at this point that I decided that as a prolegomena to the Philosophy of Inculturation, it might be useful, first, to examine what the Pope, the official teacher of the Church teaches on inculturation. On reading Pope John Paul II 's works, the "idols of ignorance" as it were, seemed to have fallen off my mind. I became conscious, that all previous teachings on evangelization have been superseded. I found in his thought, the dawn of "a new era of evangelization," a return to the original with new fervor. My own mind suddenly became organized. The principle of evangelization as understood and applied by

Pope John Paul II became the organizing principle for the detached, mosaic, fragmented and disjointed parts of my knowledge and beliefs about evangelization. It gave a unity to my thought. I then became more determined to investigate the mind of the Pope on the subject of inculturation.

The search for ideas took me to the Catholic University of America, Washington, D.C., in September 1995, at the beginning of my sabbatical leave. I walked into the Pope John Paul II Center for Marriage and Family, at the Catholic University, in search of resources. Here I met Rev. Sister Sarah Doser, the Director of the Center. After I introduced myself, I went further to inform her that I had a proposal to do a book project on Pope John Paul II's notion of inculturation. She looked expressionlessly enthused about the idea. After she read my proposal, she said "You are right, this is an important subject and a concern of the Holy Father. The Holy Father is a man far ahead of his times. Most people do not understand him." These remarks further convinced me that I had the challenge of making the mind of the Holy Father known and understood on the subject of inculturation.

The concept of inculturation has in the past two decades assumed a center stage in Afro-Asiatic theological discourse and in missiological studies in Europe and in North and South America. Inculturation, in a more general sense, is here understood as both an act and a process by which a new cultural form emanates from or is perceived in an already existing one. But, in specific Christian theological discourse, Pedro Arrupe, a one time Superior of the Society of Jesus (SJ), defined it as "the incarnation of the Christian life and the Christian message in a particular cultural context, in such a way that this experience not only finds expression through elements proper to the culture in question, but becomes a principle that animates and unifies the culture, transforming and remaking it so as to bring out a new creation."

Initially inculturation was considered a "mission church" or a Third World problem, centering on proving and showing that the gospel is at home in every culture and among all peoples, and that all peoples could maintain their cultures that were not at variance with the gospel and be authentic Christians without losing their cultural identity. But in recent times, the concept has emerged as the most promising and effective model for evangelization in all cultures of the world. How for example, is the Christian message to be presented to developing nations in an age of the search for cultural identity, and how can the same goodnews be presented to the high-tech and fast changing cultures of the "developed" nations?

Scholars like Pedro Arrupe, Joseph Blomjours, A.A.Roest Crollius, Eugene Hillman, Pope John Paul II, Teresa Okure, Peter Sarpong, Peter Schineller, Robert Schreiter, Aylward Shorter, Justin Ukpong, etc., have argued for the universalization of inculturation as a basic theological model that is applicable anywhere the Christian message is to be proclaimed. Peter Schineller, in his argument examines the Latin American Liberation theology as a contemporary example of inculturation. However, none of these scholars except Pope John Paul II seems to have offered a theoretical justification for inculturation and its universality.

The term inculturation may be new in theological texts, but its practice is as old as Christianity itself. From the Acts of the Apostle through the Apostolic times (*Didache*), through the first great missions of the Church into the outer reaches of the Roman Empire, from the Church Fathers of both East and West (Basil, Gregory, Origin, Tertullian, Ambrose and Augustine), there is unanimity on the legitimacy and practice of inculturation. However varied the methods may be, there is no doubt that the Church regards inculturation as her traditional method of fulfilling her missionary vocation to the peoples and cultures of the world.

At the time of Vatican II, "*Aggiornamento*" and "Dialogue" were crucial terms used to designate the adaptation and interaction between the Church and the world, between the Christian communities, and between Christianity and other religious traditions. During the time of Pope Paul VI, the term "evangelization" emerged to describe the perennial mission of the Church in sharing the goodnews. With Pope John Paul II, the term inculturation assumed prominence in evangelization discourse.

According to Herve Carrier, the Secretary of the Pontifical Council for Culture, John Paul II is the first Pope to speak explicitly of inculturation. It must be noted here that in the arena of creativity, when ever new words are coined and emphasized, they usually point to new ways of seeing and interpreting reality. The question is, what is the new way of seeing reality that Pope John Paul II proposes in his definition of inculturation as "the incarnation of the gospel (goodnews) in autochthonous cultures, at the same time the interpretation of those cultures into the life of the

Introduction

Church"? (*Slavorum Apostoli*, 1986). One of the new insights in this formulation is the issue of *reciprocity* in the relationship between incarnation, inculturation and evangelization. Another aspect is the theme of the *transcendence* of the word of God (goodnews), a transcendence that enables it not to be bound by any one particular culture but that enables it to incarnate in all cultures.

Given the importance of the concept of inculturation in today's theologising and its prominence in Pope John Paul II's encyclicals and addresses, it is surprising that particular attention has not been given to the systematic and textual study and critical analysis of the views of Pope John Paul II on inculturation. The closest attempts to my knowledge are the works of Andre~ Frossard, *Portraits of John Paul II,* (1990); Biffi, et al, (ed), *John Paul II: A Panorama of His Teaching*, (1989); Richard Hogan and John LeVoir, *Covenant of Love: Pope John Paul II on_Sexuality, Marriage and Family in the Modern World*, (1992); A. McCormack, *The Third World: The Teaching of Pope John Paul II,* (1984); and Ralph Martin and Peter William, *John Paul II and The New Evangelization*, (1995). But none of these focuses specifically on the analysis of John Paul II's conception of inculturation.

The purpose of this text therefore is to undertake a philosophical and critical analysis of Pope John Paul II's conception of inculturation with the hope of clarifying and thematizing his views on the subject.

The method of study will be by textual analysis of Pope John Paul II's encyclicals and addresses and, of course, his earlier works before he became pope.

Chapter One focuses on the definition of the term and its evolution. Chapter Two will trace the development of the concept of inculturation in the thought of Pope John Paul II and at the same time offer a unified theme of his encyclicals. Chapter Three will try to show how inculturation and evangelization are related. Such themes as, creation as inculturation, incarnation as inculturation, incarnation as evangelization, and evangelization as inculturation will be examined.

In Chapter Four the text will dwell specifically on what Pope John Paul II says about the new method of evangelization, namely, evangelization by inculturation. Chapter Five will then try to demonstrate how Pope John Paul II does not only teach about inculturation but that in his person and actions, he is a symbol of inculturation.

The remaining chapters will be a reflection on what could be regarded as the philosophy of inculturation. Chapter Six will examine the relationship between hermeneutics and inculturation, with the hope of showing that hermeneutics is the most rational foil for understanding inculturation. Chapter Seven will show how the notion of inculturation brings to the fore the logic of identity and universality. Chapter Eight will be the conclusion.

It is important to mention here that the text might appear repetitive to the reader. This is not because of an oversight. Rather, it is due to the hermeneutical character and overlapping nature of the themes discussed. The repetition is also purposeful and thematic. When for example, what had been said in the previous chapter is repeated, it is for the sake of emphasis and linkage to show

how what is being said in the new passage is inculturated in what had been said previously. The old is being brought forward in the new.

This text, apart from helping to clarify the concept of inculturation will help provide a focus for theologians and missiologists in their effort to propose inculturation as a universal paradigm for the process of evangelization. As a philosophical method, the concept can serve as a unifying principle which could usher in a new world order (intellectually and socially), wherein diversity of culture will be an instrument of cooperation and unity. Philosophical endeavors will no longer be viewed as activity whose task is aimed at cultural imperialism but an engagement whose aim is to discover the various manifestations of reality as are embedded in the varied cultures.

Thus through inculturation, Christianity will become not a formula but a destiny, not an ideology but a task, not a utopia but a direction that enables us to see in others what we see in ourselves, and see in ourselves what we see in others. It is only when this has happened that the true Christian community will have been built through out the ends of the earth.

CHAPTER 1

WHAT IS INCULTURATION?

Inculturation as a phenomenon in the process of human civilization is as old as man himself. But the concept and its subsequent thematization first came into prominence through Christian theologians' attempt to explain and to universalize the Christian message in all cultures of the world. The command to go and preach the gospel (goodnews) to all nations was and is interpreted as a mandate to make Christianity a universal religion. In the presence of the varied cultures of the world, how was this mission to be achieved? First imposition, then adaptation, then indigenization were all adopted as models. But these, did not seem to yield much fruit in the achievement of the divine master's plan, since every step was either met with opposition or was always confronted with new awareness or revival of cultural independence. However, with the emergence of contextual theologizing as a method, it became increasingly necessary that Christ and the Christian message be seen to be immanent in every culture. This gave birth to the thematization of the age old phenomenon and practice here referred to as Inculturation.

Definition

Inculturation in a more general sense is understood as both an act and a process by which a new cultural form emanates from or is perceived in an already existing one. But, in a more specific Christian theological discourse, Pedro Arrupe, a former Superior General of the Society of Jesus (SJ) defined it as:

> the incarnation of the Christian life and of the Christian message in a particular cultural context, in such a way that this experience not only finds expression through elements proper to the culture in question, but becomes a principle that animates, directs and unifies the culture, transforming and remaking it so as to bring out a new creation.*1*

Here Arrupe defines it specifically in relation to incarnation and the Christian message (gospel) and evangelization. Pope John Paul II shares Arrupe's understanding and defines Inculturation as "the incarnation of the gospel (goodnews) in autochthonous cultures, at the same time, the introduction of those cultures into the life of the Church."*2*

Here John Paul II does not only define inculturation within the context of incarnation, the gospel and evangelization, he also introduces something new in his definition. The new element is the introduction of reciprocity in the relationship between incarnation, inculturation and evangelization. He did this by acknowledging that while inculturation is the incarnation of the gospel in autochthonous cultures, it is at the same time the introduction of these cultures into the life of the Church. It is this insight that has earned him the recognition as the Father of Inculturation.

Evolution of the Term

Pope John Paul II may not have been the first to use the word inculturation but certainly he was the first to baptize its usage by adopting it for the first time is an official church document.

For one to understand how Pope John Paul II came to use the word and the difference that there is between the earlier usage and the way he has employed the term, it is useful that we trace briefly the history of the origin and usage of the term.

Pope John XXIII, the man who opened the windows of the Church to let in fresh air, was also the man who initiated the Second Vatican Council, which eventually opened the doors of the Church giving birth, as it were, to the renewed mission of the Church *Ad Gentes*. He, it was who discouraged the mono-cultural perception of the Church and affirmed a Church of Christ that transcends a given culture. In his *Princeps Pastorum* he stated:

> the Church does not identify herself with any particular culture, not even European and Western culture, which her history is so closely linked... Rich is her youthfulness which is constantly renewed by the Holy spirit, the Church is ever ready to recognize, to welcome and indeed to encourage all things that honor the human mind and heart even if they have their origin in places of the world that lie outside the

Mediterranean basin which was the providential cradle of Christianity.3

Enthused by this official papal openness to other cultures, and the discussions that were taking place at the then ongoing Second Vatican Council, scholars began to investigate new ways by which the Church can reach out to other cultures. In 1962, J. Manson published an article *L'Eglise Ouverte Sur Le_Monde* - The Church Opened to the World. In this article, he used the expression "Catholicisme Inculture~."4 According to Oliver Onwobiko, this expression was theologically significant in that it placed "*inculture~*" within the context of religion, *catholicisme*, and culture.5 *Inculture~* - inculturation here was concerned with the dialogue between Christianity and culture through the Church.

During the First Plenary Assembly of the Federation of Asian Bishops' Conference in 1974, the terms "inculturate" and "inculturated" were used extensively and often in relation to incarnation. Their final document included such statements as "the local church is a church incarnated in a people, a church indigenous and inculturated."6 In 1977, Cardinal Sinn of Manila, who had been a key actor at the Asian Bishops conference, used the term inculturation at the Synod on Catechesis in Rome to convey the feelings and perceptions of the Asian bishops on how to bring the goodnews to the Asian people. Pedro Arrupe in his own contribution at the same 1977 Synod, noted that to impose foreign cultural forms on a people who have their own culture as the only possible way of expressing the faith and living it, can be an obstacle to catechesis. He pointed out that the cultural crisis in Europe shows that inculturation is not to be understood as something applicable only to non-European cultures, but to European cultures also. Catechesis according to him presupposes the inculturation of the faith because catechesis is the result of an inculturation and also a constant dynamic instrument of inculturation.7

By the end of 1977, the term inculturation had definitely assumed a center stage in missiological discussions. On May 14, 1978, Arrupe addressed a letter titled "*On Inculturation*" to the members of his Society. In this letter, he instructed them that the period of "surface adaptation" is gone, that inculturation was to become their watch word and emphasis in their missionary activity. In this same letter, he touched on crucial aspects of inculturation, namely, its applicability and universality. He wrote:

> It is clear that the need for inculturation is universal. Until a few years ago one might have thought that it was a concern only of countries or continents that were different from those in which the Gospel was assumed to have been inculturated for centuries. But the galloping pace of changes in these latter areas ... persuades us that today there is need of a new and continuous inculturation of the faith everywhere. The concepts, "missions", "Third world", "East/West", etc., are relative and we should get beyond them, considering the whole world as one single family, whose members are beset by the same varied problems...8

Furthermore, in responding to the question on the notion of inculturation he wrote:

> Inculturation is the incarnation of Christian life and of the Christian message in a particular cultural context, in such a way that this experience not only finds expression through elements proper to the culture in question, but becomes a principle that animates, directs and unifies the culture, transforming and remaking it so as to bring about "a new creation".9

What is evident in the quotations cited above is that Arrupe did not only associate inculturation with incarnation and evangelization but also saw it as a method of evangelization that had universal applicability in all cultures. In the same year 1978, the year that Karol Cardinal Wojtyla became Pope John Paul II, Roest Crollius published an article, *What is So New About Inculturation?* In this article, he further expanded the understanding of inculturation within the Jesuit tradition and explored the contribution that inculturation can make towards the universalization of the Church. He wrote:

> Inculturation of the church is the integration of the Christian experience of a local church into the culture of its people, in such a way that this experience not only expresses itself in elements of this culture, but becomes a force that animates, orients and innovates this culture so as to create a new unity and communion, not only within the culture in question but also as an enrichment of the church universal.*10*

This idea of inculturation bringing about "a new unity and communion", and "enrichment of the church universal" was definitely a novel idea.

It was within this period that most notable theologians such as Karl Rahner began to use the term in their theological reflections and writings. In an article he published in 1979, he wrote: "Christianity must inculturate itself if it is now to be, as it has begun to be, genuinely a world Church."*11* This, one could say, was a cautious engagement in a concept that was still to be fully accepted in the language of the Church. Despite this caution, Rahner still ended up with a defense of the cultural autonomy of the local churches, with the argument that a certain amount of independence in cultural spheres of the local churches will be a measure of how far the local church is "inculturated and no longer a European export."*12*

John Paul II became Pope in 1978. There is no doubt that he was very familiar with the discussions on inculturation before he became Pope. He was an active participant, representing the Polish church at the 1977 Synod of Bishops, where discussions on inculturation dominated every agenda. He was personally aware of the necessity of inculturation in the evangelizing mission of the Church. He was also aware of the newness of the use of the term and the need to give it a proper and definitive understanding in the language of the Church's theological discuss. When therefore he became Pope, he assumed a personal responsibility of becoming the teacher and agent of inculturation in the evangelizing mission of the Church. Even though he did not use the term in his first encyclical, *Redemptor Hominis* (1979),*13* it became clear in his later writings that inculturation was to become the matrix for the achievement of what he had proposed in that first encyclical.

Six months after the publication of *Redemptor Hominis*, he published an apostolic exhortation, *Catechesi Tradendae*. Here he dwelt on inculturation extensively and used the term to designate a process of evangelization. A process that will offer the different cultures the "knowledge of hidden mystery and help them to bring forth from their own living tradition, original expressions of Christian life."*14* This idea of bringing forth from the peoples' living tradition, original expressions of Christian life is an indication that John Paul II had a clear vision of the idea of Christ and his message incarnating in the cultures of the various peoples of the world. It was for the reason of this understanding that he noted emphatically in the *Catechesi Tradendae*(no.53), that although the term "inculturation" may be a neologism, "it certainly expresses very well one factor of the great mystery if incarnation".

This concept became the major subject of his evangelization speeches and sermons. In 1980, during his first visit to Africa, he addressed the African bishops in Zaire on the necessity of inculturation. He said:

> One of the aspects of this new evangelization is the inculturation of the gospel, the Africanization of the church ...This is part of the indispensable effort to incarnate the message of Christ....15

Here Pope John Paul II clearly indicates a vital relationship between evangelization, inculturation and incarnation by arguing that inculturation is an aspect of evangelization and an indispensable process of incarnating the message of Christ. Later, in the encyclical *Redemptoris Missio*, he will defend incarnation and evangelization as forms of inculturation. In the same year, in Nairobi, Kenya, he spoke of inculturation thus:

> Inculturation, which you rightly promote, will truly be a reflection of the incarnation of the word, when a culture, transformed and regenerated by the gospel, brings forth from its own living tradition original expressions of Christian life.16

Still, in the same address he persuades the African bishops not to be afraid of inculturation because:

> ...there is no question of adulterating the word of God or of emptying the cross of its power (1 Cor. 1:17) but rather of bringing Christ into the very center of African life and of lifting up all African life to Christ. Thus not only is Christianity relevant to Africa, but Christ, in the members of his body, is himself African.17

It might be interesting to note here the consistency of Pope

John Paul II's thought. It is exactly what he had written in the exhortation, *Catechesi Tradendae*, that he is now preaching to the African bishops. Nothing could be more persuasive and revealing of the Pope's intent on what he means by inculturation than his admission that Christ is incarnated as African.

The theme of seeing a unity and relation between evangelization, inculturation and incarnation is to become the core of Pope John Paul II's missionary endeavor. For example, in his *Familiaris Consortio* (1981), he speaks of inculturation in the context of marriage and the family. *18* In January 1982, while addressing the National Congress of the *Movement Ecclesial d'Engagement Culturel*, he argued for the need to evolve a dynamic synthesis between culture and faith. He rested his argument on inculturation as the matrix for the possibility of such synthesis. *19*   In 1985, during the Extraordinary Synod of Bishops, he sought to draw a distinction between the earlier evangelization by adaptation, and that by inculturation. He said:

> Inculturation is different from simple external adaptation, because it means the intimate transformation of authentic cultural values through their integration in Christianity in the various human cultures. *20*

The emphasis here is on internal transformation of cultures which by implication can be effected only by Christ himself. How this takes place and what the Pope intends here will be fully discussed in the section on Inculturation and Evangelization.

It was in the encyclical *Slavorum Apostoli* (1985), that the Pope gave what has come to be accepted as his definitive definition and summation of his concept of inculturation. Here he defined inculturation as:

the incarnation of the Gospel message (the Good News) in
autochthonous cultures, at the same time the introduction of
those cultures into the life of the church.*21*

This definition apart from highlighting the notion of
reciprocity brings out the essence of the transcendence of the
word of God, a transcendence that is manifest in its ability to
be incarnate and made seen in all cultures. It is this ability of
not being bound by one particular culture that enables it to be
found in all cultures, and the basis of the universality of the
word of God. This definition also entails a new kind of
understanding of the burden of evangelization. The
evangelizer is now to go about identifying and proclaiming
Christ who is already present in all cultures. The aspect of
"introducing those cultures into the life of the church" is an
invitation to universalize the presence and the message of
Christ as it manifests itself in these cultures. The new forms
that have been identified must be recognized and accepted as
being part of the many faces of the universal church.

The new vision of evangelization through inculturation
necessarily entails not only an epistemological shift but also an
ethical practice. A new way of seeing and understanding, and
a new way of acting. Although Pope John Paul II himself
admits, that this task is not an easy one, he nonetheless
encourages us, not to be afraid to imitate the Divine Master.
In his address to the Pontifical Council for Culture (1987), he
highlighted this problem when he said:

> You are aware that inculturation commits the church to a path
> that is difficult, but necessary. Pastors, theologians and the
> specialists in the human sciences must also collaborate
> closely, so that this vital process may come about in a way
> that benefits both the evangelized and the evangelizers, in

order to avoid any simplification or undue haste that would end in syncretism or a secular reduction of the proclamation of the Gospel. Carry out your research on these questions serenely and in depth, aware that your work will help many in the church - and not only in what are called "mission lands".*22*

Here, apart from noting the difficulty of, and the diligence with which inculturation is to be handled, the Pope touches on the idea of reciprocity in the relationship between the evangelized and the evangelizer. The two must necessarily benefit in the inculturation process.

By 1990, the term inculturation had become a household word among theologians and missiologists. It was no longer unusual for the term to be used in official church documents. The most prominent of such documents was the *Lineamenta of the Special Assembly of Bishops for Africa.23* This document tries to develop a history of inculturation. Citing some of the relevant passages here will enhance our understanding of what the document intends:

Traces of an effort toward which might be called inculturation might already be detected in the first preaching of the Gospel by the Apostles. Like the covenant of old, the apostolic tradition comes to us in various writings each of which bears the imprint of its author and that of the community to which it owes its origin. All, however, safeguard the essential unity of the unfathomable mystery of Jesus (Eph. 3:8). The evangelists, for example, present their Gospel to us from different perspectives and with different but complementary accents, marked by the "Life situation" of their respective ecclesial communities. For the sacred authors wrote the four Gospels, selecting some things from the many which had been handed on by word of mouth or in writing reducing some of them to synthesis, explicating some things in view of the situation of their churches, and preserving the form of proclamation but always in such fashion that they told us the honest truth about Jesus.*24*

Another section of the *Lineamenta* reads:

> Inculturation or the process through which the Christian faith
> is incarnated in cultures is bound by its nature to the
> proclamation of the Gospel. This is explained by the fact that
> inculturation is rooted in the incarnation of the word of God
> (*Logos* `word').... That is why the announcement of the gospel
> does not hesitate to employ contemporary expressions from
> culture: indeed, through a certain analogy with the humanity
> of Christ, they are required in order to be said in this way to
> share in the dignity of the divine word itself. Because the
> cultures in Bible history have been judged capable of being
> vehicles of the word of God, for this reason something very
> positive can be found which is already a presence "in germ"
> of the divine word. It is not a work of transforming
> Christianity into "culturalism"...another thing is to be of
> service to a culture, or retranslate it in new words and in new
> perspective the traditional Gospel teaching... Also every
> church (sent to the nations) witnesses to its Lord only if,
> having consideration for its cultural attachments, it conforms
> to Him in the first *kenosis* of His Incarnation and in the final
> humiliation of his life-giving passions. Each culture ought to
> be evangelized in the light of the Gospel and purified of its
> negative elements.*25*

Here the document definitively relates inculturation to
incarnation and vice versa and also affirms the fact that
incarnation had and has affected all cultures. Thus, witnessing
to the Lord by every church must be in relation to "having
consideration for its cultural attachment" and conforming to
Christ "in the first *kenosis* of his incarnation."

It was in this same year, 1990, that Pope John Paul II
published what could be regarded as his *magnum corpus* on
inculturation - the Encyclical *Redemptoris Missio.26* Here he
explaines his basic teaching on inculturation and traces the

process of inculturation from God the Father to God the Son, and from God the Son to God the Holy Spirit. He traces the process of inculturation in creation, incarnation and evangelization and shows how inculturation is the only rational matrix for explaining the relationship between the three (creation, incarnation and evangelization). It might be of significant interest to point out here, that Pope John Paul II draws the logic of his analysis of the relationship between creation, incarnation and evangelization on the one hand and that between incarnation, inculturation and evangelization on the other, from his knowledge of the internal logic and unity in the Triune God trinitarian relationship.

For Pope John Paul II, there is an internal unity in the relationship between the Father, the Son and the Holy Spirit. It could be reasoned as follows: In the beginning, at the moment of creation, the spirit of God hovered over the earth, then God the Father spoke the *Word:* "Let there be..." and things came to be. Thus, at creation, were present, God the Father, God the Son (the Word of God) and the Spirit of God.

At the moment of incarnation, the angel Gabriel, the messenger of God delivered the Word sent by God to Mary and the Spirit hovered over the blessed Virgin Mary and she was conceived by the power of the Holy Spirit. That which was conceived by Mary was the Word of God, and the Angel named Him Jesus, the Son of God.

Thus, the *Word* spoken by God, whether at the beginning of creation or through the Angel to Mary, was made flesh and dwelt among us. St. John's gospel puts it poetically, "In the beginning was the Word and the Word was with God and the Word was God ... and the Word became flesh and dwelt among us. "(Jn.1-18).

What can be concluded from this reasoning is that the Three Persons of the Trinity were present both at the moment of creation and at the moment of incarnation. And because of the internal logic and unity that exists between them we say logically, that as the Father is to the Son, to the Holy Spirit, so is creation to incarnation, to evangelization (A :B :C :: X :Y :Z).

These issues, of the logic and the nature of the relationship between creation, incarnation and evangelization will be discussed in detail in chapters 3 and 4.

So far what we have tried to do in this chapter, is to attempt in a sketchy manner to trace in a chronological order the emergence and the usage of the term inculturation in theological discourse and in church documents. The next chapter will try to focus on the analysis of the development of the notion of inculturation in the thought of Pope John Paul II.

References

Chapter 1

1. Pedro Arrupe,"Letter to the Whole Society on Inculturation" in Studies in *International Apostolate of* Jesuits, 2 (June 1978)
2. John Paul II, *Slavorum Apostoli*, June, 1985.
3. John XXIII, *Princeps Pastorum*, no.16.
4. J. Manson, *Eglise Ouverte Sur Le Monde*, NRT, 84, 1962.
5. Oliver A. Onwubiko, *Theory and Practice of Inculturation* (Enugu: SNAAP Press, 1992.

The King's Library

6. *Final Statement of the Federation of Asian Bishops Conference* (FABC), no.12, "His Gospel to our People ..." Vol.11, Manila, 1976, Cited A.A.Roest Crollius, "What Is So New About Inculturation" in *Gregorianum* Vol.59,1978, p.28.

7. For information about Arrupe's contribution at the Synod, I am indebted to Onwubiko, *Inculturation: Theory and Practice* p.4.

8. Arrupe, "Letter to the Whole Society..." no.7 p.9.

9. Ibid, no.2.

10. A.A.Roest Crollius, "What Is So New About Inculturation", *Gregorianum*,Vol.59, 1978, p.735.

11. Karl Rahner, "Towards a Fundamental Theological Interpretation of Vatican II" in *Theological Studies*, vol. XI, 1979, p.723.

12. Ibid., p.719.

13. Pope John Paul II, *Redemptor Hominis*, March 4, 1979.

14. Ibid., *Catechesi Tradendae*, no.53 October, 1979.

15. Ibid., *African Address*, Bologna, Editrice Missionaria, Italiana, 1981, p. 38ff.

16. Ibid., African Bishop's Challenge" no.6.

17. Ibid.,

18. Pope John Paul II, Apostolic Exhortation *Familiaris Consortio,* November 22, 1981.

19. Ibid., "Speech to the National Congress of the Movement Ecclesial d'Engagement Culturel" in J. Gremillion, *The Church and Culture Since Vatican II*, (Indiana: University of Notre Dame Press, 1985).

20. Final Report of the 1985 Extraordinary Synod of Bishops, "The Mission of the Church in the World" no.4 in *The Extraordinary Synod 1985* (Boston: St. Paul Publication, 1986).

21. *Slavorum Apostoli* June 2, 1985.

22. John Paul II, An Address to the Pontifical Council for Culture, January 17, 1987.

23. *The Lineamenta of the Synod of Bishops Special Assembly for Africa and Her Evangelization Mission Towards the Year 2000 "You Shall be My Witnesses* (Act.1:8), Vatican City, 1990.

24. Ibid., pp. 46-47.

25. Ibid., pp.48-49

26. John Paul II, *Redemptoris Missio*, December 7, 1990

CHAPTER 2

THE DEVELOPMENT OF THE THOUGHT OF POPE JOHN PAUL II ON INCULTURATION AND THE UNITY OF HIS ENCYCLICALS.

When John Paul II became Pope, he did not only inherit the name John Paul from his immediate predecessor, Pope John Paul I, but he also inherited the legacy of Pope John XXIII's pontificate, the legacy of the Second Vatican Council and that of Pope Paul VI.

Before the time of Pope John XXIII, evangelization was couched under the rubrics of imposition. The new religion or gospel was set over or imposed on the old culture. The result was that, like a seed that is planted on a rock, it never had the opportunity to take root. The problem with imposition was that it saw Christianity as a finished product that could be neatly exported from one culture to another. Everywhere the Church was perceived as something foreign. Even in places where the Church seemed to have taken root, the people felt suffocated. Definitely there was need for the Church to redefine her mission in the world. The Second Vatican Council came as a response to this yearning. Pope John XXIII, at the opening of the Council, called for the renewal of the Church - *Aggiornamento*. But the renewal, as it was understood at the time, was in terms of renewal of faith for those who had it and the renewal of the Church in countries where it already existed. This renewal saw the emergence of translations of liturgical texts and adaptation of selected liturgical forms. These meant very little for the places where the Church did not exist. According to Oliver Onwubiko, this sense of renewal led to a theology of renewing the European church and adapting it to the mission territories.*1* But, fortunately, the Second Vatican Council ended on the note of *Ad Gentes*, of converting the whole Church into the mission of God.

Pope Paul VI, who had the responsibility of closing the Second Vatican Council, opened his Pontificate with the encyclical, *Ecclesiam Suam*, "Church what do you have to say about yourself?" The Second Vatican Council Dogmatic Constitution on the Church, *Lumen Gentium*, answered the question by defining the Church as an "evangelizer" and called for a new kind of evangelization wherein the laity will assume a responsibility both in holiness and in their responsibility in the mission of the Church.*2*

Within a period of about 15 years, evangelization moved through many phases. From translation and adaptation to indigenization, then from contextualization to the era of incarnation theology.*3* With the incarnational theology, a new stage was set for a new understanding of evangelization that came to be known as inculturation.

Pope Paul VI championed the course of the new evangelization. He was the first Pope to make apostolic journeys to other continents. During his Pontificate, he visited about sixteen countries. These included the Holy Land(1964), India (1964), USA- New York (1965), Portugal (1967), Ephesus (1967), Columbia (1968), Geneva (1969), Uganda (1969). In 1970 he visited eight other countries. Among these were: Tehran, East Pakistan, the Philippines, West Samoa, Australia, Indonesia, Honkong, and Sri Lanka. With this break with the tradition of a stationary Pope, Pope Paul VI sent a powerful message, that the mission of the Church is to carry the message to the ends of the world.

Drawing inspiration from the work of the Council, Pope Paul VI devoted his pontificate to the task of evangelization. In 1967, he renamed the Congregation for the Propagation of the Faith the Congregation for the Evangelization of Peoples. In 1974, he published his encyclical *Evangelii Nuntiandi* (EN) - *On Evangelization in the Modern World*, in which he exhorted the people to accept evangelization as the "deepest identity of the Church, which exists in order to evangelize."4 He called for a positive and effective evangelization of all cultures. According to Pope Paul VI:

> ...what matters is to evangelize man's culture and cultures (not in a purely decorative way, as it were by applying a thin veneer, but in a vital way in depth and right to their roots).5

In another passage, he said:

> ...evangelization loses much of its force and effectiveness if it does not take into consideration the actual people to whom it is addressed, if it does not use their language, their signs and symbols, if it does not answer the questions they ask, and if it does not have an impact on their concrete life.6

Here Pope Paul VI clearly indicates that the new evangelization focuses on the evangelization of man's culture and cultures, and that it must have an impact on the concrete life of the people.

What seems to emerge so far is that with Vatican II and Pope Paul VI, evangelization had assumed a new understanding and orientation. In Vatican I for example, which took place in the early 19th Century (1869 - 1870), the term gospel (evangelium) was used only once. Even at that, the term was used with reference to the written gospels and not to the gospel message. 7 During Vatican II, the word gospel was used 157 times and the verb "evangelize" 18 times and the noun "evangelization" 31 times. However, when Vatican II used evangelization it meant the proclamation of the basic Christian message of salvation through Jesus Christ and was usually with reference to individual conversion. 8

Pope Paul VI's *Evangelii Nuntiandi*, opened a new dimension of evangelization , namely, the evangelization of cultures. The document also described the Church not only as the evangelizer but also as that which is to be evangelized. "The Church is an evangelizer, but she begins by being evangelized herself."9 Thus, even with Pope Paul VI, evangelization was already seen as an activity that involves both inward and outward processes. This was the historical station of the Church at the time that John Paul II became Pope.

Karol Cardinal Wojtyla, a prominent leader and spokesman of the Polish church, who later became Pope John Paul II, was an active participant in the Second Vatican Council sessions and in the formulation of the final documents. He new perfectly well what the feelings and the thinking of the Church were on the subject of evangelization. When therefore he became Pope, his primary concern was on how to bring to fulfillment the spirit and aspirations of the Council on the mission of bringing the goodnews to the ends of the earth. He found the answer in a doctrine centered on Christ. He saw in Christ the Redeemer of the world, who penetrated in a unique and unrepeatable way into the mystery of man and entered his "heart."

Apart from his ecclesiastical heritage, Pope John Paul II also had an academic heritage which gave clarity to his thought and shaped his world view. As a 20th Century philosopher and theologian, he was schooled in the Lublin/Cracow phenomenological tradition. A background that brought about not only a new kind of synthesis between faith and reason in his mind but in his perception and understanding of man and his vocation. At the heart of this new synthesis is the concept of personhood. In his conception, he stresses the irreducible value of the human person.

The development of his thought can be traced to his earlier published works: *Love and Responsibility* (1960), *The Acting Person* (1970), and *Sources of Renewal* (1972). For Pope John Paul II, man is a person because he is like God, "made in the image and likeness of God." As analyzed by Richard Hogan and John LeVoir, "if a man is made in God's image, then his only hope, if he is to be true to his very self, is to function as God intends."*10* For John Paul II, therefore, the revelation of God, especially the revelation shown to man by the incarnation is thus essential if man is to be true to his own self. Incarnation, one might say, is the revelation of the ideal man in the true image of God. Through incarnation, the son of God unites himself with each man. In a sense, therefore, incarnation as a mission is evangelical, it invites man to be his fullness, that is , return to his original state. In the Pope's thought, man is created in the image and likeness of God. But the likeness was tarnished at the fall. Christ who is the new man is the perfect image of God. Man can realize his true image or personhood only through believing in Christ and living a Christ-like life. Without Christ in a man's life, such a man is no man. Following this same line of reasoning Hogan and LeVoir said:

> Original sin made it impossible for us to live and act as God intended. We could no longer function as human beings because we could no longer fulfill the role for which God had created us. We need Christ to make it possible for us again to live as images of God ... Christ restores creation and is therefore "the center of the universe and of history."*11*

The Pope's notion of inculturation provides a framework for understanding the relationship between creation, incarnation and redemption. Evangelization by its very nature is an invitation to man to return to himself and function as the image of God. One could see in this discourse of the thought of Pope John Paul II, two fundamental hermeneutical progressions: one beginning with God and moving toward man, and the other beginning with man and moving toward God. The result is the unity of incarnation and inculturation, God becoming man and man becoming divine, a unity that restores man to his original state, and restores the original relationship between God and man, and man and God.

With a rich and unique intellectual heritage, such as has been cited above, it is not surprising that Pope John Paul II has emerged as the most prolific Pontiff that has ever occupied the Chair of Peter. The publication of his recent book, *Crossing the_Threshold of Hope*, makes him the first Pope to enter the world of literary essays, dropping the formality of the *Magisterium.*

In the eighteen years of his pontificate, Pope John Paul II has published twelve encyclicals and several other exhortations and addresses. Five of these encyclicals form the core and unity of his teaching. These are: *Redemptor Hominis* (March 4, 1979), *Dives in Misericordia* (November 30, 1980), *Dominum et Vivificantem* (May 18, 1986), *Redemptoris Missio* (December 7, 1990), and *Ut Unum Sint* (May 25, 1995). Each of these encyclicals will be analyzed with the hope of highlighting the central theme or thread that ties and connects or links them together. Such a central theme will be shown to be the core of Pope John Paul II's teaching.

In the *Redemptor Hominis*, the first of his encyclicals, he reflected on the mystery of Christ who is the redeemer of man. One of the unique themes about the redeemed man is that it is the concrete individual man who is redeemed and not man in some abstract sense. But, he soon found out that the redemption could not have been possible without the generous love and mercy of God the Father. This awareness led to the writing of the *Dives in Misericordia*, where he demonstrated that it is through the mercy of God the Father whose gratuitous nature necessitated the sending of the Son. With this encyclical, John Paul II had retraced his steps and returned to the origin of the universe - the story of creation. He showed how God the Father in his love created man in His image and likeness. But man refused his friendship and sinned, and fell short of grace. Still God the Father in His divine mercy sent his Son to redeem man. This redemption would not be effected unless Christ in his person was a perfect image of God that was originally in man at the first moment of creation. Here the Pope established a direct link between creation and incarnation.

God the Son having been sent by the Father entered human history, identified with man. Because of this identification he was able to effect a redemption which merits him the name, *Redemptor Hominis*.

The opening section of the *Redemptor Hominis* is titled *Inheritance,* and the opening sentence of this first section indicates the source and direction of John Paul II's pontificate and ministry. The sentence reads:

> The redeemer of man, Jesus Christ, is the center of the universe and of history. To him go my thoughts and my heart in this solemn moment of the world that the church and the whole family of the present-day humanity are now living....*12*

And further, in the same section he added:

> God entered the history of humanity and as a man, became an actor in that history... Through the incarnation God gave life the dimension that he intended man to have from his first beginning.*13*

Here we see Pope John Paul II defining the thrust of his ministry. His heritage is incarnational and he relates this incarnation event directly to what God intended man to be at the first moment of creation - created in the image and likeness of God. No wonder, then, Pope John Paul II had to return to the beginnings by showing how creation is related to incarnation. He maintains that "there is a link between the first fundamental truth of incarnation and the ministry ... that has become his specific duty as the successor of Apostle Peter."*14* Drawing from the prayer of Christ in St. John's Gospel, "I pray ... that they may be one" (Jn.17:21) he shows how incarnation aims at restoring all things in Christ.

It might be of value to note here that Pope John XXIII had preached the necessity of Christian unity. The Second Vatican Council responded with its Decree on Ecumenism as a means of reaching out to the separated brethren. Pope Paul VI in his encyclicals *Ecclesiam Suam* and *Evangelii*

Nuntiandi, laid emphasis on the necessity of dialogue in evangelization. He showed how creation was a manifestation of how God dialogues with himself -"Let us make man in our own image and likeness." When man fell, God sought to restore him. Incarnation for Paul VI was the way that God dialogued with his creature, a means by which God sought to restore man to grace. Evangelization therefore was seen by Pope Paul VI as the Church dialoguing with the world to bring salvation to all.

At the end of the pontificate of Pope Paul VI, and the short term of Pope John Paul I, the question then arose: "How was this dialogue to be brought about in the new age, such that Christian unity can be achieved?" This question rested on the shoulders of Pope John Paul II when he himself asked:

> How, in what manner should we continue? What should we do
> in order that this new advent of the church connected with the
> approaching end bring us closer to him whom the scripture calls
> "Everlasting Father."15

He responded by seeking a return to the origins of primary evangelization. He sought to give a new meaning to what Pope Paul VI tried to explain with the concept of dialogue. With Pope Paul VI, dialogue had meant a negotiation between two or more persons or ideas, wherein the two autonomous persons or ideas, maintain their positions but seek to enrich themselves through a process of give and take. Pope John Paul II, unlike his predecessor, sought to understand dialogue in terms of *kenosis,* a self emptying such as was effected by Christ in the incarnation and redemption. As noted by Archbishop Honore~ in his commentary on the *Redemptor Hominis,* and the mystery of redemption, Pope John Paul II is not so much interested in giving explanation of the dogmas (of the church) but in putting them in perspective, that is, in

showing the internal logic of the revelation that orders them
one to the other, seeking to define how they are related, and
to bring to light their significance with regard to salvation. *16*
The challenge of Pope John Paul II, therefore, was to propose
a way of explaining how creation is related to incarnation and
how incarnation is related to evangelization. Thus, with Pope
John Paul II, what Pope Paul VI called dialogue was to have
a new understanding and a new methodology. A new
understanding concerning how creation relates to incarnation
and how the great mission of revealing Christ to the world, of
helping each person to find himself in Christ (evangelization)
rests on the capacity to discover Christ and Christian value(s)
that is already sown in every individual by virtue of
incarnation. *17* Because of his deep seated belief in the
universality of the effect of incarnation, he concluded and still
believes that a true missionary (evangelical) attitude begins:

> with a feeling of deep esteem for "what is in man", for what
> man has himself worked out in the depths of his spirit
> concerning the most profound and important problems. It is
> a question of respecting everything that has been brought
> about in him by the spirit, which "blows where it wills." *18*

Definitely Pope John Paul II was charting a new course
of evangelization in seeking to respect that which is already in
man and that which has been brought about in man by the
spirit. This definitely is a reference to man's cultural
inheritance. He also noted in the same text that evangelization
does not mean "destruction" of what was already there, but a
"taking up." According to him, evangelization "is never a
destruction; instead, it is a taking up and fresh building, even
if in practice there has not always been full correspondence
with high ideal." *19*
    In the encyclical *Redemptor Hominis*, Pope John Paul

II makes a distinction between what he calls the "divine dimension" and the "human dimension" of the mystery of redemption.*20* Creation and Incarnation belong to the divine dimension while evangelization belongs to the human dimension. However, it must be pointed out that the human dimension is derived from, rooted in and linked to the divine dimension or mission. Evangelization at the human level would not be, if it were not a continuation of that which was initiated by the divine at creation and continued by the incarnation. For the Pope, therefore, it is God who first initiates human history through creation. And the redeemer of the world reveals "in a new and more wonderful way the fundamental truth concerning creation."*21* Incarnation thus represents God's further intervention in human history.

Even though Pope John Paul II never used the word inculturation in this first encyclical, from the analysis done so far of the text, one can see, *ab initio*, that he was really in search of a deeper understanding of the internal mechanics and logic of the relationship between creation, incarnation and evangelization.

In October 1979, six months after the publication of *Redemptor_Hominis*, while writing his Apostolic exhortation *Catechesi_Tradendae*, Pope John Paul II found a word which seemed to have captured the essence of what he tried to describe in his first encyclical. The word was "Inculturation." It was in this document that the word inculturation first and formally appeared in an official Papal document. As Herve Carrier, the Secretary of the Pontifical Council for Culture, noted, Pope John Paul II was and is the first Pope to speak explicitly of inculturation.*22*

Pope John Paul II was so fascinated by his discovery of the notion of inculturation, that he admitted openly in the text, that he finally found a word which "expresses very well one factor of the great mystery of the Incarnation."*23* Without any reservations, he associated inculturation with incarnation and incarnation with inculturation. He also in the same text related inculturation to evangelization by asserting that it is a process that:

> ...will offer the different cultures the knowledge of hidden mystery and help to bring forth from their own living tradition original expressions of Christian life.*24*

Another revolutionary vision of John Paul II in this exhortation is the movement from the evangelization of the individual to the evangelization of cultures as a precondition for the redemption of both man and his culture. Since man, at least in part, is a product of his culture, if his culture is divinized, he too will be absorbed in the divinity. Thus the thrust towards the evengelization of culture is envisioned as the most pragmatic way of redeeming the whole of man.

On June 2, 1980, while addressing UNESCO in Paris on a paper titled "Man's Humanity is Expressed in Culture," the Pope took time to explain what he means by culture.*25* He began his analysis by first of all rejecting the popular conceptions of culture. As noted by Alessandro Maggiolini, Bishop of Como, Italy:

> John Paul II does not limit himself to the conception of culture as the generic refinement of mind, and as a consequence of this refinement, products such as works of thought, art, science, and so on. Nor does he identify culture with information or · erudition. Still less does he join the school of thought that indiscriminately opposes "culture" to nature ... still less does he adopt the point of view of a certain "structuralism" according to which the person as a responsible subject does not exist, culture would be a system of convictions and customs which would exist in so far as they arise from a collectivity co-ordinated in

time and/or space.*26*

Pope John Paul II rejects all these prevailing definitions. In his own understanding, he sees man as both the subject and object of culture. He sees man as a thinking and free subject, joined with matter, but at the same time transcends matter by his spiritual dimension. From his attempt to perceive a unity of both the divine and the human culture in man, he finds it difficult to offer a definition that can accommodate both the divine and the human dimensions. However, he finally defined a cultured man as:

> the person who expresses himself, thinks and acts, who creates certain behavior, and by these is helped or hindered in his efforts to become fully what he should be - namely the image and likeness of God.*27*

Thus, for Pope John Paul II, since the human culture in an ideal sense has its foundation in the divine, a true human culture must be an extension of the divine culture. A cultured person then, would be one who seeks or relives his original culture or way of life. In the Pope's understanding, the ideal original culture of man is the divine culture (man was and is made in the image of God) which is rooted in Christ. So, for him, to be cultured is to be Christ-like.

What John Paul II intends in his new method of evangelization is that the divine be discovered in the human culture. His evangelization strategy is a search for the unity or oneness of both the divine and human cultures. This is what Christ had achieved at the incarnation.

In Pope John Paul II's address to the African bishops in 1980 in Zaire, he sought to practicalise his theory of the relationship between incarnation and culture. He told the bishops that "one of the aspects of evangelization is the inculturation of the gospel, the Africanization of the church."28 This he says "is part of the indispensable efforts to incarnate the message of Christ."29 In the same year in Kenya, he told the African bishops in no uncertain terms that the new method of evangelization was imperative. He told them that they must "bring Christ into the very center of African life" and thereby lift up "all African life to Christ." By this process Christianity will not only be relevant to Africa but "Christ, in the members of his body , reveals himself as African."30

Whatever the African bishops understood this to mean, one thing was certain, the Pope was advancing a new theory of evangelization based on the concept of inculturation.

At the general audience of September 8, 1982, the Pope returned to the original theme of the relationship between creation, incarnation and the Church. In this address, he pointed out a new internal relationship which is based on sacramentality. He spoke about the original order of grace that proceeds from the "sacrament of creation" and referred to incarnation as the sacrament of redemption.31 Still, in the same address, he spoke of "the mystery of Christ and the Church, which gives the Church it's sacramental aspect." During the September 29, 1982 Audience, he spoke of the "mystery of creation" that must be understood fundamentally "as a making visible of the invisible." And at the October 6, 1982 Audience, he stated that "the holiness originally bestowed on the human person by the creator is part of the reality of the 'sacrament of creation'." Here the notion of creation, incarnation and the Church participating in the same sacramental character reveals the development of the Pope's thought on the internal unity that exists in the creation - incarnation - church relationship.

On March 9, 1983, he gave an Address to the Latin America Bishops. In this address, he told them of the new evangelization which is "new in expression, new in fervor and new in its method."*32* The question is what was this new expression, new fervor and new method of evangelization that the Pope was talking about? It was still yet to be defined. In 1985, during his Address to the Extra-Ordinary Synod of Bishops, Pope John Paul II sought to draw a distinction between the earlier evangelization by adaptation and dialogue, and that which he advocates through inculturation. He stated: "Inculturation is different from simple external adaptation, because it means the intimate transformation of authentic cultural values through their integration in Christianity in the various human cultures".*33* By this distinction, he clearly indicated that his method was different from that of his predecessors. The significant thing about this new method is that it involves an intimate and internal transformation of the culture and it also involves the integration of this transformed culture into Christianity.

By way of perhaps appealing to authority or some empirical evidence of what he was advocating, he published on June 2, 1985, the encyclical *Slavorum Apostoli*. Here he gave an example of how the kind of evangelization through inculturation which he was proposing had already and successfully been achieved by SS. Cyril and Methodius in their evangelization of Eastern Europe (the Slav people). He noted how their method "contains both a model of what today is called `inculturation' - the incarnation of the gospel in native cultures - and also the introduction of these cultures into the life of the Church."*34* In his example, he cited how Cyril and Methodius did not:

> ...seek to impose on the people assigned to their preaching either the undeniable superiority of the Greek language and Byzantine culture, or the customs and way of life of the more advanced society in which they had grown up and which

necessarily remained familiar and dear to them. Inspired by the
ideal of uniting in Christ the new believers, they adapted to the
Slavic language the rich and refined texts of the Byzantine
liturgy and likewise adapted to the mentality and customs of the
new peoples the subtle and complex elaboration of Greco-
Roman law.*35*

In another passage he said:

The Brothers from Salonika were not only heirs of faith but also
heirs of the culture of Ancient Greece, continued by Byzantium
.... Their pioneering work of evangelization among the Slav
peoples is both a model of what today is called "inculturation" -
the incarnation of the Gospel in native culture - and also the
introduction of these cultures into the live of the church.*36*

What we have here is a reference to a typical example of the
synthesis of the gospel and culture. So, in a sense, Pope John
Paul II's proposal of inculturation as a way of synthesizing the
gospel and culture is not really new. It is only an attempt to
reintroduce and universalize that which was practiced in a
particular church according to the ancient tradition of the
Apostles.

Having now defined and ostensibly shown what he
meant and means by inculturation, he proceeded in the
following year (February 3, 1986) to discuss the issue of
liturgical inculturation, emphasizing the need to inculturate the
liturgy from within the people's cultural experience.*37*

With the conviction that this new method of
evangelization is in keeping with the divine process, and that
no meaningful inculturation can be achieved without the
direction of the Holy Spirit, he then wrote and published the
encyclical on the Holy Spirit, *Dominum et Vivificantem* (May
18, 1986). Here he discussed the role of the Holy Spirit in the
life of the Church. He acknowledged that the Holy Spirit

continues to direct the redemptive work of the Father and the Son in the world. In this encyclical, he showed how, through incarnation the love of God is identified with an active presence of God in the hearts of men. He also argued that it is through incarnation that the efficacy of the original creation is restored and similarly that it is in the mission of the Holy Spirit that the Son who had "departed" in the paschal mystery, comes back, and is always present in the mystery of the Church.38 Commenting on John 16:7, "If I go, I will send the advocate to you," he established a linkage principle between the sending of the Son and the sending of the Holy Spirit.39

For Pope John Paul II, as it was for Pope Paul VI, the Holy Spirit is the principal agent of evangelization. "Through the Holy Spirit the Gospel penetrates to the heart of the world."40 Pope John Paul II notes the fact that it was through the power of the Holy Spirit that the Virgin Mary conceived and incarnation became a reality. Mary was filled with the Holy Spirit. Thus, when she visited Elizabeth with the goodnews, at the sound of her greetings, the child in Elizabeth's womb, filled with the Holy Spirit, leapt for joy. (Luke I: 42ff). Jesus was led by the Holy Spirit to the desert and was led by the Spirit to the river Jordan to be baptized and witnessed to by John the Baptist. After the Baptism of Jesus, we are told that the heavens opened and the Holy Spirit descended on him and a voice came from heaven saying: "this is my beloved Son...." (Luke 3: 21-22). In a sense, we can say that it was the Holy Spirit who showed Jesus to the world. There is no doubt that the Holy Spirit is the principal agent of evangelization and the Holy Spirit still continues the work of making Christ manifest in the Church today.

Having completed the analysis of the relationship between the Father, the Son and the Holy Spirit in the economy of human salvation, Pope John Paul II still had a

thorny theological issue to resolve. This was the problem of
the role of Mary the mother of Christ in the salvation history.
How was the Blessed Virgin Mary to be placed in the
economy of this new evangelization process? This led to the
writing of the encyclical *Redemptoris Mater* (May 3, 1987).
Here he reflected on Mary and her role in the economy of
salvation. He showed how Mary was the first to be redeemed
as a precondition for her to be a fitting vessel for the
incarnation process. God the Father sent the Angel Gabriel to
her. She was hovered over by the Holy Spirit. Incarnation was
effected. Thus , in her was present the mission of the Father,
the Son and the Holy Spirit. Mary, the human object was
redeemed. Her own redemption was completed. And because
her redemption was completed while still being in the human
form she was called blessed even by the Angel.

It is in this sense that Mary is the new Eve - the
redeemed woman, and Christ - the new Adam. While the old
Adam and Eve disobeyed God the Father, both Christ and
Mary, the new Adam and Eve submitted to the will of the
Father. Mary said: "Be it done to me according to your will."
Christ in his own response to the Father said: "Into your
hands, I commend my spirit." Thus Mary became the first
"truly human" to be redeemed. She is the first among equals
"Primus inter pares." Perhaps this is one of the rational
justifications of the doctrine of the Assumption of the Blessed
Virgin Mary. Since her own redemption had been completed,
she had no need of passing through the way of mortals but be
taken body and soul to heaven.

For Pope John Paul II, therefore, Mary has a place in
the economy of salvation. She is the "Mother of the
Redeemer." The Pope also sees in Mary a symbol of
inculturation. At the moment of incarnation, when Mary was
chosen as the instrument, God did not seek to change her, but

rather, redeemed her by making her worthy of her call as the mother of the Redeemer. It was an internal spiritual transformation.

The definition of the role of Mary in the new evangelical movement seemed to have been the last hurdle that Pope John Paul II had to overcome before outlining the method and the strategy of the new evangelization. Three years after the publication of the *Redemptoris Mater*, he published the *Redemptoris Missio* (December 7, 1990). In this encyclical, he showed how the work of the Triune God is continued in the Church and how the Church is mandated to participate and bring to fruition the mission of the Triune God. The Pope wrote:

> God is opening before the church the horizons of a humanity more fully prepared for the sowing of the gospel. I sense that the moment has come to commit all the church's energies to a new evangelization and to the mission *Ad Gentes*. No believer in Christ, no institution of the Church can avoid this supreme duty: to proclaim Christ to all peoples.*41*

In another passage he said:

> Today as never before, the church has the opportunity of bringing the Gospel, by witness and word, to all people and nations. I see the dawning of a new missionary age, which will become a radiant age bearing an abundant harvest, if all Christians ... respond with generosity ... to the calls and challenges of our times.*42*

Here he links the new effort of evangelization with the preparation for the Third Millennium of Christianity and calls on all to view the 1990's as "an extended Advent season in preparation for the great Jubilee of the Incarnation."*43* But before the great Jubilee, Christ is to emerge in all cultures.

Creation itself is groaning for manifestation. The Jubilee itself will be the manifestation of a greater presence of Christ. The challenge of the new evangelization is to discover Christ already present in the world.

How is this mission of the Church to be achieved? The encyclical focuses on the human dimension of the divine mission - evangelization. Here he returns to the original evangelization movement - the creation - incarnation relationship. He discovers that the one thing that is common in every stage is the inculturative process. He then proposes inculturation as the definitive method in the evangelization life of the Church.

It is in this encyclical, *Redemptoris Missio*, that he articulates fully his doctrine of inculturation in relation to the major moments of salvation history such as creation, incarnation and evangelization. He wrote:

> As she carries out missionary activity among the nations, the church encounters different cultures and becomes involved in the process of inculturation. The need for such involvement has marked the church's pilgrimage throughout her history, but today it is particularly urgent. The process of the church's insertion into peoples' cultures is a lengthy one. It is not a matter of purely external adaptation, for inculturation means the intimate transformation of authentic cultural values through their integration in Christianity and the insertion of Christianity in the various human cultures. The process is thus a profound and all embracing one, which involves the Christian message and also the church's reflection and practice....
>
> Through inculturation the church makes the Gospel incarnate in different cultures and at the same time introduces peoples, together with their cultures, into her own community. She transmits to them her own values at the same time taking the good elements that already exist in them and renewing them from within. Through inculturation the church, for her part

becomes a more intelligent sign of what she is, and a more effective instrument of mission....
Inculturation is a slow journey which accompanies the whole of missionary life. It involves those working in the church's mission *Ad Gentes*, the Christian communities as they develop.

Missionaries, who come from other churches and countries, must immerse themselves in the cultural milieu of those to whom they are sent, moving beyond their own cultural limitations. Hence they must learn the language of the place in which they work, become familiar with the most important expressions of the local culture, and discover its values through direct experience. Only if they have this kind of awareness will they be able to bring to the people the knowledge of the hidden mystery in a credible and fruitful way.*44*

Pope John Paul II has said it all in the quoted passage. Here he addresses such themes as creation as inculturation, incarnation as inculturation and inculturation as evangelization. The central theme that he also develops, is seeing creation and incarnation as being evangelical. Another very powerful insight that is brought to bear in this encyclical is the issue of reciprocity in the relationship between incarnation, inculturation and evangelization. What is more, that the evangelizer is to bring the people to the knowledge of the hidden mystery points to the aspect of Christ being present yet unrevealed. He is hidden in the people and in their culture. The issue of the transcendence of the word of God is also a major feature in evangelization. A transcendence that enables it not to be bound by any one particular culture but that enables it to incarnate in all cultures.

    In the section where he wrote about inculturation in relation to mission *Ad Gentes* and the Christian communities, he clearly distinguishes three types or stages of inculturation. The first stage, which is mission *Ad Gentes,* has to do with mission to the whole world. The second stage which has to do with pastoral care is concerned with the faithful Christian communities. The third stage has to do with re-evangelization of those who had initially been evangelized but have lost faith. These stages can also be seen to be similar in form to the mission of the Father - *Ad Gentes*, of the Son - pastoral care, and of the Holy Spirit - re-evangelization.

Finally, Pope John Paul II sees the mission of the Church as being in keeping with the mission of God the Father, God the Son and God the Holy Spirit, namely that "all may be one," that all may be restored as one through Christ to God the Father. Since incarnation had affected all, they must all be harvested as one and restored to the Father.

It was this awareness that necessitated the writing of the encyclical *Ut Unum Sint*. "That they may be one" is the theme of this encyclical. The unity in question is the unity which the human race with all its variety has "from God and in God." This unity is rooted in the mystery of creation and it receives the new dimension of universal salvation with the mystery of redemption.45 In this encyclical the Pope expressed his hope and vision of the Year 2000 and invites all Christian to take into account the ecumenical promise (that all may be One), especially, as we are at the threshold of the Third Millennium.

All other encyclicals or exhortations and addresses are either further explanations of the essential teachings of these five encyclicals or reflections on how the life of the rediscovered or redeemed man in Christ affects the different facets of human life whether private or social. For example, in the *Laborem Exercens* (September 14, 1981), he discussed the value of human work, how human work is a participation in the divine work. He showed how the value of human work is more important than the dimensions of capitalism and collectivism which seem to render man at the service of work instead of work being at the service of man. Because of the dignity of human labor, he argued that all economies must be at the service of man. It might be noted here, that the *Laborem Exercens*, was really the Pope's response to the problems of the labor union in Poland. Even though the Pope was under pressure to respond to the situation that the Solidarity Movement was facing in Poland at the time, he successfully weaved his message under the umbrella of his general papal teaching. Thus giving the encyclical a universal applicability. This conjecture seems to be consistent, given the fact that at the time the *Laborem Exercens* was published, it seemed to have been an interjection into the Pope's program of thought. After John Paul II had written the first and second encyclicals, *Redemptor Hominis* (1979) and *Dives in Misericordia* (1980) respectively, the next, following the sequence of thought should have been the *Dominum et Vivificantem* (1986), but this was not the case. His thought was interrupted by the Solidarity problem and he had to address the immediate problem, and this led to the publication of the *Laborem_Exercens* (1981) as the third encyclical.

The next encyclical, which is an application of his central teaching, was the *Sollicitudo Rei Socialis* (December 30, 1987). This encyclical deals with the duties of society and government in promoting the common good. Societies and governments that do not rule on the basis of Christian values of justice, love and fairness says the Pope, are heading for doom. Man can neither understand himself nor achieve his goal unless he follows the Christian way. The common good of man and the society is the glory of God and service of man.

In the *Redemptoris Missio*, as earlier mentioned, he outlined the method and strategies for the new evangelization. For the new evangelization to achieve its purpose, human culture must be harmonious with the Christian values. 46 As a follow up to this encyclical, he published the *Centesimus Annus* (1991), where he argued for the role of culture in evangelization.*47*

In 1993, he published the *Veritatis Splendor*, where he defended the need to recognize the objective moral principles which are rooted in God, who alone is the truth. The truth of God is revealed in no other than Christ who said "I am the Way, the Truth, and the Life" (Jn. 14: 6).

The *Evangelium Vitae* (March 25, 1995) is his gospel of life. Here he defends the sacredness of life and the respect it deserves. The sacredness of life stems from its being the image and likeness of God. He then links the new effort of evangelization with the preparation for the Third Millennium of Christianity and calls on all to view the 1990's as "as extended advent season in preparation for the great jubilee incarnation."*48* But before the great jubilee which he anticipates in the *Ut Unum Sint* (May 25, 1995), Christ is to emerge in all cultures. Creation itself is groaning for manifestation. The jubilee itself will be a greater manifestation of the person and presence of Christ. The new evangelization therefore must be centered on the person of Jesus Christ, and the one and eternal gospel.

One thing that is certain in all these encyclicals is that they are all rooted in the person of Christ and his mission in the world. It is only in him that all things, all human activities and all human beings find meaning. Another feature of the encyclicals which depicts the inherent unity in the works, is that they are centered on the trinitarian relationship of Father, Son and the Holy Spirit and their mission in the world. How the mission begins with the Father who creates in love, and who in his mercy sends the Son to redeem a fallen man. The Father and the Son together send the Holy Spirit who in turn ensures that all things are restored to the Father through the

Son.

The thing that is novel and unique about John Paul II's treatment of this trinitarian relationship is that he interprets their relationship as involving a type of inculturation. Thus inculturation images as the organizing principle in all of Pope John Paul II's teaching on creation, incarnation and evangelization.

References

Chapter 2

1. Oliver Onwubiko, *Theory and Practice of Inculturation*, (Enugu: SNAAP Press, 1992) P.10.

2. Vatican II Council Document, *Lumen Gentium*, no.7

3. For a more detailed study of the different phases of evangelization, See Peter Schineller, *A Hand Book on_ Inculturation*, New York: Paulist Press, 1990, pp.14-21.

4. Pope Paul VI, *Evangelii Nuntiandi*(EN), no.14, 1974.

5. Ibid., no.20.

6. Ibid., no.63.

7. Dogmatic Constitution, *Pastor Aeternus*, Ch.1, DS, 3053.

8. Ralph Martin and Peter William, *Pope John Paul II and the_New Evangelization*, (San Francisco: Ignatius Press, 1995), p.26.

9. Evangeli Nuntiandi, no.15.

10. Richard M. Hogan and John M. LeVoir, *Covenant of Love: Pope John Paul on Sexuality, Marriage, and Family in the Modern_World*, (San Francisco: Ignatius Press, 1992), p.33.

11. Ibid., p.35. This notion of Christ being "the center of the Universe and

History" is borrowed from Pope John Paul II. See *Redemptor Hominis*, no.1.

12. Redemptor Hominis, no.1.

13. Ibid.,

14. Ibid., no.2.

15. Ibid., no.7.

16. Archbishop J. Honore~, "Christ the Redeemer, Core of John Paul II's Teaching" in *John Paul II: A Panorama of His_Teachings*, (New York: New City Press, 1989), p.13.

17. Redemptor Hominis, no.11.

18. Ibid., no.12.

19. Ibid.,

20. The distinction between "divine dimension" and "human dimension" is further highlighted by Honore~. See *John Paul_II: A Panorama of His Teachings*, p.16.

21. Redemptor Hominis, no.8.

22. Herve Carrier, "Inculturation: A Modern Approach to Evangelization" in *Inculturation in Nigeria, Proceedings of the Bishops Study Session on Inculturation*, (Lagos: Catholic Secretariate of Nigeria Press, 1989), p.4.

23. Catechesi Tradendae, no.53.

24. Ibid.,

25. Ibid., See also, "Man's Entire Humanity is Expressed in Culture", Address to UNESCO, Paris, June 2, 1980.

26 Alessandro Maggiolini, "Faith and Culture in the Teaching of John Paul II", in *John Paul II: A Panorama of His Teachings*, pp.161-162.

27. Cited by Maggiolini, in *Panorama*, p.162.

28. John Paul II, "African Bishops Challenge" no.6 in *African_Addresses*, Bologna, 1981.

29. Ibid., Address to African Bishops in Kenya, 1980.

30. Ibid.,

31. John Paul II, "General Audience", September 8, 1982.

32. Ibid., "The Task of the Latin American Bishops", Address to CELAM, March 9, 1983, *Origins* 12, (March 24, 1983), p.661.

33. Final Report : D "Mission of the Church in the World" in *Extraordinary Synod*, 1985 (Boston: St. Paul Publication, 1986).

34. Slavorum Apostoli, no.21.

35. Ibid., no.13.

36. Ibid., no.21.

37. See *Osservatore Romano,* February 3, 1986.

38. John Paul II, *Dominum et Vivificantem,* no. 63, May 18, 1986.

39. Ibid., no.25.

40. Evangelii Nuntiandi, no.75.

41. John Paul II, *Redemptoris Missio,* no.3 December 7, 1990.

42. Ibid., no.92.

43. Avery Dulles, "John Paul II and the New Evangelization - What does it Mean", in Martin and Williamson, *Pope John Paul II and the New _ Evangelization,* p.28.

44. Redemptoris Missio, nos.52-53.

45. Hans Cardinal Groer, "The Church: Sacrament of Salvation", in *Panorama,* p.36.

46. More will be said on this in the chapter on Inculturation and Evangelization.

47. John Paul II, *Catesimus Annus,* no.50.

48. Avery Dulles in Martin and Williamson, *Pope John Paul II and the New Evangelization,* p.28.

CHAPTER 3

INCULTURATION AND EVANGELIZATION

The question of how inculturation is related to evangelization and vice versa is a very complex one. Inculturation by its very nature dates back to the creation event and spans through incarnation to the Church's missionary activity - evangelization. Evangelization as it is understood in this text takes its root from the incarnation event and extends to the Church's missionary activity. Creation is related to incarnation as inculturation is related to evangelization, and similarly, creation is related to inculturation as incarnation is related to evangelization.

It is recommended, that to have a better understanding of the relationship between inculturation and evangelization, one begins with the initial themes such as: Creation as inculturation, incarnation as inculturation, incarnation as evangelization, evangelization as inculturation.

3.1 Creation And Inculturation

What we call creation in its primordial sense is a

"distancing" or an "externalization" of an aspect of the divine way of life (culture). This divine way of life includes the act of creating. Creation therefore could be defined as the act of bringing to being that which was hitherto not in its present mode of existence. Creation thus can be seen as God extending his being in otherness. By creating, he causes the human nature to be. A mixing of the divine nature with the creaturely nature. It is an internal activity that results in otherness.

The word creation can also be used with reference to the product of the creative act. This is the sense of which the whole of the created order is sometimes referred to as creation.

There are two types of creation. Creation out of nothing - *Creatio ex nihilo* and creation by which something is fashioned out of an already existent material. Creation out of nothing is applicable only in the case of a divine act.

The end result of creation can be in reference to some material and physical object or it could refer to an immaterial or non material objects as in the case of the creation of ideas or musical creation.

Whatever form creation takes, the significant thing is that the process is inculturative.

The word culture, a term from which inculturation is derived is itself a very difficult word to give a precise definition. But in a very simplified though comprehensive form, the word is often used with reference to a way of life. It could refer to the sum total of a peoples' way of life or it could be used with reference to a particular or specific aspect of the peoples' way of life.

This way of life or culture is often brought about by the process of translating one's idea of life into words/or actions. Where the words and actions serve as a means of communication, a language is evolved. Where this language and/or action becomes habitual, a way of life has evolved. It is this systematically evolved way of life that is often referred to as culture.

Inculturation therefore, in a general sense refers to a process by which a new way of life (culture) is brought out of an existent culture. Or to put it differently, one could describe it as the emergence of a culture from within a culture. When for example, God said, "Let there be ...," and things came to be, it was the word of God that was made manifest in creation. Thus by creation, a new culture other than the divine culture was brought into being. This new culture was the culture of the created order.

The same is also true of the event that took place when God said "Let us make man in our own image and likeness." By this utterance, God self-emptied himself as a result of which the human culture was created. The "let us make man" is a divine decision, in which God, as it were, wills to become involved in creation in a more intimate and intense way. Creation here is the work of God alone. He does not only make man but makes him in his own likeness. "To our own image and likeness" indicates a type of correspondence. According to Cardinal Lo~pez, the Hebrew term *selem* which is translated as *image*, denotes a correspondence between something created and the original model. The human being therefore has been created according to the form, the archetype, the image of God.*1*

The human being is a creature caught up in a dialogue of life with God. Creation is the outcome of a dialogue, and the human life is a life of continuous dialogue with God. Pope John Paul II in his General Audience in December 1978 noted as follows:

> The fact that man is made in the image and likeness of God
> means, among other things, that he is capable of receiving
> God's gift; that he is aware of this gift, and that he can respond
> to it. Precisely for this reason God, from the beginnings
> established an alliance with man and with man alone *2*

It is in this sense of God's self emptying as a result of which something new came into existence, that creation is a form of inculturation. Through creation, a new way of life emerged. The word of God was inculturated or became incultured. With this understanding of creation as the bringing to being of a new way of life (culture), and of inculturation as the emanation of a new cultural form from an existing one, creation can be seen as a perfect form of inculturation.

3.2   Incarnation And Inculturation

Incarnation is here understood as a manifestation of the divine in a human culture. The divine lets itself be seen and experienced in and from within the human culture. Thus the Scripture says, "the word became flesh and dwelt among us" (Jn.1:14). According to Peter Schineller, the most directly theological word to express the meaning of inculturation is incarnation.*3* Pedro Arrupe shares a similar opinion when he wrote: "the incarnation of the son is the primary motivation and perfect pattern for inculturation.*"4*

Incarnation thus refers primarily to the entire Christ-event - the coming, birth, growth, daily life and struggle, teaching, healing, resting, celebrating, suffering, dying, and rising of Jesus Christ. In incarnation, God became man. God neither adapted himself nor adapted man. He simply, as St.John says, became man and dwelt among us. Jesus was born, lived and died a Jew. He was called a Nazarene (Matt.

2:23). He expressed the truth and the love of the living God through the Jewish language and customs. When incarnation took place in the Jewish culture, what emerged did not have a parallel from which it was to be reconciled. It was a self transforming activity after which what emerged was still a Jewish culture. Teresa Okure of the Catholic Institute of West Africa, Nigeria, summarized this incarnation experience succinctly when she wrote:

> The theological basis for understanding of inculturation lies in the provision made by God Himself in creation, in the mystery of the incarnation - redemption (the Christ -event, the Paschal mystery)... From the moment of its creation, all of humanity was destined for God, since it was created "in the image and after the likeness of God"(Gn.1: 26). When humanity forfeited this divine destiny through original sin , God in Christ , in the fullness of time (Gal.4:4) became incarnate in order to assume, transform from within, save and restore humanity and creation itself to its original destiny, and reconcile it with himself (Rom. 8:18-30; 2Cor. 5:19).5
>
> Jesus' self emptying was followed by a taking on of our humanity through the normal process of conception by a woman (Gal. 4:4), birth, growth and learning (Lk. 2:51-52). As a human being, Jesus accepted in toto the finite conditions of our human existence (Heb. 4:15). This assumption of humanity was a demonstration of deep love and "a feeling of deep esteem" for what is human 6

If we take the incarnational christology seriously, we cannot but take example from the divine creation. When God said "Let there be" things without exception came to be. When God said "let us make man", He initiated the creative process of all human race without exception. By this very creative act, all human race and cultures were touched. It was from this that St. Thomas Aquinas derived his cosmological argument for the existence of God, wherein all creation points to the possibility of an uncreated Creator.

In the same vein, incarnation affected all the human race, it penetrated and elevated all human cultures. It is in the light of this universal incarnation that Herve Carrier affirmed that "faith in Christ is not a product of any culture" rather that "its origin lies in a divine revelation which is already immanent and inherent in every culture."7 Schineller shares the same understanding when he wrote:

> Revelation, God's self-communication takes place in and through cultures. Thus to understand the God who reveals and the self-communication offered, we must pay attention to the historical context or culture. Cultures, both traditional and modern, remain the locus for God's past, present and future revelation.8

Pope John Paul II, in his address to the university community at the University of Coimbra, Portugal, echoed this same understanding of the relationship between incarnation and inculturation. He stated:

> It is through the providence of God that the divine message is made incarnate and is communicated through the culture of each people. It is for ever true that the path of culture is the path of man, and it is on this path that man encounters the one who embodies the values of all cultures and fully reveals the man of each culture to himself. The gospel of Christ, the incarnate word finds its home along the path of culture and from this path it continues to offer its message of salvation and eternal life.9

Here John Paul II, in no uncertain terms, defends the position that incarnation is only possible within the context of culture. Besides, this culture in question is not one universal culture but the culture of each people. It is also important to note his position that it is Christ who reveals the man of each culture to himself. This incarnate word finds its home in every culture and continues to offer its message of salvation. Here the Pope admits that incarnation through inculturation is not a static event, rather, it is dynamic and continuous. The same understanding between incarnation and inculturation was echoed in the *Catechesi_Tradendae*, when he stated that although "the term inculturation may be a neologism, it expresses very well one factor of the great mystery of the incarnation."[10] Thus, in Pope John Paul II's address to the Kenyan Bishops, he noted emphatically that inculturation must be understood as the effort to communicate the message of Christ by incarnating it in the lives and cultures of each people, thereby enabling them "to bring forth from their own living tradition original expressions of Christian life, celebration and thought."[11]

The Nigerian bishops in their Joint Pastoral Letter on *Inculturation,* taking a queue from the Pope also expressed the same view when they wrote:

> There is no culture no matter how perverse, which does not possess some positive structures, symbols and value systems as imprints of God's passage through her ... The event of the incarnation does not belong entirely to the past. Rather its historical essence is of a re-occurring nature, making it possible for the *logos* to continually assume the body of any subsequent human history and culture. This is why incarnation is used synonymously with inculturation.[12]

Here the Nigerian bishops seem to appeal to the Genesis experience, where everything that was made by God was seen to be good. Despite the fall, there was still some inherent goodness in all that were made by God. It was and is, this inherent goodness that allowed for the possibility of redemption and restoration. The Nigerian bishops are therefore   consistent in stating that there is no culture, no matter how perverse, which does not possess some imprints of God's passage through her. If this were not the case, then incarnation would not have been both a cosmic and a universal event.

In another place, the Nigerian bishops also admitted that incarnation is an adequate model of inculturation, basing their argument on the fact that incarnation is a cosmic event that encompasses the entire human history.*13*

The implication of the notion of incarnation as inculturation is that there is no one culture which is the embodiment of the message of Christ. Rather, all cultures, as in creation, were and are affected simultaneously by the incarnation event and thus all cultures are immanently transformed.

Given this understanding, the task of evangelization is the proclamation of the universal transformation by Christ that has already been effected. With incarnation therefore, inculturation had at the same time been initiated and perfected, not as something that has been finished and done with, but as a continuous process that is constantly actualizing itself.

This is the same kind of understanding that the Council Document *Ad Gentes* intended when it argued:

> If the church is to be in a position to offer all the mystery of salvation and the life brought by God, then it must implant itself among all these groups in the same way that Christ by his incarnation committed himself to the particular social and cultural circumstances of the men among whom He lived.14

The conclusion therefore is that, with the understanding of inculturation as the process of emanation of a new cultural form from an already existing one, incarnation can be seen as a perfect form of inculturation. This is why this text had earlier described Pope John Paul II's definition of inculturation as "the incarnation of the gospel message in autochthonous cultures" as the most insightful, pragmatic and philosophically profound definition. This definition implies a seeing of the incarnation event as having affected all cultures. Thus, making the function of the evangelizer, a matter of going about, identifying and proclaiming Christ who is already present in a given culture. The aspect of "introducing these cultures into the life of the church" is an invitation to universalize the presence and message of Christ as it manifests itself in these cultures. The new form that has been identified must be recognized and accepted as being part of the many faces and facets of the universal Church. This aspect of seeing and proclaiming is what is often referred to as evangelization. The text will therefore proceed to examine the relationship between incarnation and evangelization.

3.3 Incarnation And Evangelization

The fall of man brought a debased nature to man. Despite this debasement, God did not abandon man. He still wanted him to be redeemed. He sent his son to assume the human nature so as to reclaim it for Himself. This sending of the son and the assumption of the human nature is what is often referred to as incarnation - God becoming man. The divine culture enters into the human culture, assumes it and makes it whole again. Christ did not change the human nature or culture but assumed it as it was and is. Thus, restoring man to his original state.

This is the evangelical mission of incarnation. Evangelization is here understood as the proclamation of

God's salvation to man. Christ effectively achieved this by ensuring that all human race was affected by his act. Christ himself admitted that the proclamation and establishment of God's Kingdom was and is the purpose of his mission. "It was for this purpose I was sent" (Lk. 4:43).

Pope Paul VI, in his apostolic exhortation *Evangeli Nuntiandii*, affirmed the existence of "a profound link between Christ, the Church and evangelization. *15* "As the Father sent me, so am I sending you" (Jn.20:21).

By incarnation, death and resurrection, Christ had completed his salvific act. What remains is for the Church, whose mission is to continue the work of Christ, to go about identifying and harvesting the fruit of the salvific act of Christ. The Church's missionary work is that of a harvester. This is why Christ prayed to the Father to send laborers because the harvest is plentiful. Christ had seen the effect of the incarnation in the universe. What remains is for the Church to harvest all back to God the Father. How is this harvesting to be achieved? This is the task of evangelization.

The central focus of incarnation is God becoming man. "The word became flesh and dwelt among us" (Jn.1:14). And so, after the word had been made flesh, the Magi, the Shepherds, went and saw the child in Bethlehem and recognized in him, the messiah that was to come and did him homage. Thus, through incarnation, the divine lets itself be seen and expressed in and from within the human culture. As noted by Pope John Paul II, through incarnation God gave human life the dimension that He intended man to have from the first beginning. *16*

Inculturation, like incarnation is a phenomenological experience and has therefore to be accompanied essentially by a looking, a seeing, and a recognizing. Inculturation began by God becoming man and the second stage of inculturation was the recognition by humans of the divine intervention in human history. Inculturation and incarnation would not have been known to be unless it was recognized as such by man. It is this continuous recognition of the presence of God in human culture and history that both historicizes and actualizes the original inculturation (incarnation). Jesus himself re-emphasized this in St. Matthew's gospel when he narrated the parable of the kingdom on the last day. He said:

> ... Lord when did we see you and gave you water to drink, ... as long as you did it to the least of your brothers, you did it to me .... Lord when did we see you and did not give you water to drink ... as long as you did not give it to the least of your brothers, you did not do it to me. (Matt. 25: 25ff)

Here Jesus universalizes incarnation. The failure of the second group is that they saw Jesus but could not recognize him while the glory of the first group lies in their ability to have seen and recognized that Jesus was alive even in the needy.

Incarnation as it relates to inculturation has a challenging implication for evangelization. The ability to recognize Christ who is already present is crucial for effective evangelization. Preaching therefore is to be characterized by the proclamation of the Christ that manifests himself in the peoples' culture and history. This is exactly what John the Baptist, the first proclaimer did. "Behold the Lamb of God ... This is he whom I said `after me there comes one who has been set above me, because he was before me.'" (Jn.1:29-30).

Jesus also emphasized *beholding* as a major task in the spreading of the goodnews. Jesus said "Blessed are your eyes because they have seen." For those who have no faith Jesus said, "You will look and look but you will not see , You will listen and listen but you will not hear." Here *seeing* and *hearing* are presented as being essential to evangelization.

Could we then say that the failure of the evangelizers to see Christ in other cultures is due to their faithlessness?

At the birth of Christ, the Magi were invited to come and see the Messiah. Nathaniel was invited by his brother Philip to *come* and *see* the Messiah. Philip said: "We have found him of whom Moses in the Law and the Prophets wrote ... 'come and see'" (Jn. 1:45-48). The sense of finding (found him) which Philip emphasizes points to the fact that the Messiah was already present but unknown to the people. He needed to be made known. Jesus himself said "to have seen me is to have seen the Father" (Jn. 14:8-12). The Father is made manifest in the incarnate Son. Just as the Father is made manifest through the Son, the divine message of salvation is made manifest through the human culture. Pope John Paul II expressed this thought very well when he said:

> Since the seeds of the word are found in all cultures, we must look and behold the signs of the goodnews that are present in human culture, be it African, Asia or Europe. If we do not discover them, then it is either we have no faith or we are overlooking the creative presence and challenge, the richness of the mystery of God's presence throughout human history and culture.*17*

This theme of *looking* and *beholding* the signs of the goodnews is very crucial to the understanding of the new notion of evangelization through inculturation. He (the pope) like Christ admits that the failure to see the presence of Christ is due to lack of faith.

Jesus also opened another dimension of this incarnational evangelization when he said: "Whoever *acknowledges* me before others, I will acknowledge him before my Father in heaven" (Matt.10:32-33). Here *acknowledgement* is introduced as an essential ingredient of evangelization. It is not enough just to look and see, one must proclaim what he has seen. This is the essence of bearing witness to Christ.

The word evangelization is the noun form of the verb "to evangelize." It has its root meaning from the Greek word *euaggelizo* which means "to announce the goodnews." This preaching of the goodnews according to Justin Ukpong of the Catholic Institute for West Africa, means announcing to all nations, the breaking in of the divine rule on earth.[18] Evangelization therefore means the proclamation of the goodnews of God's salvation to all people. This proclamation stirs up faith and brings about the fulfillment of salvation (Rom.1:16ff; Phil.1:27).

What necessarily comes to mind here is the question of the relationship between evangelization and inculturation. The *Lineamenta* describes inculturation as "encounter of the gospel with all cultures of the world, or better still, the encounter of the goodnews with all the peoples of the earth through the instrumentality of their culture."[19] It goes on to affirm that "the announcing of the gospel to all peoples of the earth is inconceivable without inculturation."[20] What seems to follow here is that, since the "announcement of the gospel is not possible without inculturation, and since in the order of being , inculturation must take place before the gospel could be known and proclaimed, evangelization must be ineluctably linked to inculturation. It must also be pointed out, that in the order of knowing and proclaiming, inculturation and knowledge of, and proclamation, both inculturation and evangelization take place at the same time. As already discussed, the dynamics of evangelization as a process of inculturation lies in the capacity of the "evangelizer" to see and recognize the elements of the goodnews in the culture which he beholds. The moment he proclaims what he recognizes, evangelization has taken place. The evangelizer becomes a witness to the fact that the goodnews had and has been inculturated from the first moment of incarnation. The moment that the evangelized believes in what has been proclaimed salvation is fulfilled or actualized.

The conclusion, therefore, is that incarnation itself is an evangelizing act. And what we call evangelization in the Church's missionary activity is really the actualization of, or bringing to fulfillment that which was and is initiated by Christ himself.

3.4   Evangelization And Inculturation

This is an aspect of inculturation that has often been misunderstood. Most missionaries and evangelizers, and writers on evangelization often think of evangelization as a "carrying of the goodnews" to " some cultureless" people. A type of *tabula rasa* concept approach. This notion is incorrect. From what has been said of inculturation and evangelization so far, it is almost certain that the task of evangelization lies in the ability of the evangelizer to recognize the elements of the goodnews that are already present in a given culture and to proclaim their presence to all in the territory. The messengers message is to be found among the people to whom he is sent. The experience is like that which was experienced at the resurrection of Christ. The women were told to carry the message of the resurrection to the disciples. But the message which they were to deliver had already gone ahead of them and they were to find him already in Galilee where the disciples were (Mk. 16:3-8). The Scripture tells us that it happened that as they were talking together and discussing what they had been told, "Jesus himself came up and walked by their side; but their eyes were prevented from recognizing him" (Lk. 24:13-16). Here is a typical example of a situation where the message is already present among the people to whom the messenger is being sent yet the message is not known to be present. Even Cleopas who was a disciple did not recognize Jesus. It was at the breaking of the bread that their eyes were opened and they recognized Jesus (Lk. 24:28-31).

The task of the evangelizer therefore is to go about searching for and proclaiming the virtue of the incarnation event. John Paul II noted this when he said: "We must give thanks for the grace of God given to each and every human being, not just to those of us here, but to every brother and sister in every corner of the world."*21* The Pope here recognizes the fact that the grace of God has already been given to all. As already argued, inculturation had already, and is still taking place by the fact of the primeval incarnational inculturation. Evangelization as inculturation, therefore, is the perceiving and the making known of, the goodnews that is already there in the peoples' culture. Or, to put it differently, the task of evangelization is the perpetuation of the primeval inculturation. It is in this context that Schineller referred to all ministers of the Gospel as "agents of inculturation".*22* It is in this sense that evangelization is an inculturation act and inculturation itself becomes an evangelization process.

A typical example of evangelization as inculturation could be found in St. Paul's *beholding* and *proclaiming* in Athens at the Areopagus (Acts. 17:1ff). Here Paul proclaims the goodnews of Jesus Christ as he perceived it from within the Greek Philosophies and culture of the day. Peter Sarpong, Bishop of Kumasi, Ghana, expressed a similar Pauline orientation when he noted at the Eucharistic Congress in Philadelphia that "African ground had long been carefully prepared by God for Christianity."*23* John Paul II echoed the same theme in his address to the Nigerian Bishops when he told them that the divine message is incarnated and communicated through culture of each people and therefore all people are called upon to proclaim it.*24* While addressing the African Bishops in Kenya, the Pope dwelt on the same theme by insisting that it is by respecting, preserving and fostering the particular values and richness of peoples' cultural heritage that they will be in a better position to lead them to a better understanding of the mystery of Christ, which is to be lived in the noble, concrete and daily experience of African life.*25* Peter Schineller in his own commentary on the subject added that it is only in and through particular cultures and contexts that God's love and truth are revealed and made present.*26*

It is within this context that faith becomes very necessary, both for the "evangelizer and "the evangelized." The evangelizer needs deep faith to be able to recognize the presence of Christ in any culture he beholds. He also needs courage to proclaim what he beholds. On the part of the evangelized, they also need both faith and courage to accept what is being manifested of them and their culture.

What must be noted here is that, the *perceiving* and *beholding* necessarily entail the rejection of those elements in a given culture that are anti-Christ or that have negative influence on the goodnews. For example, it is interesting to remember that the Word of God became flesh and was like man in all things but sin. So, Christ himself was able, in the process of proclamation of the goodnews in his life and in his words to condemn the Jewish value preferences that were antithetic to the gospel. One thing that could be learnt from Christ is that while he identified with the good and rejected the bad, he never attempted to impose something which was alien to the Jewish culture. He always drew from the Jewish tradition to support what the people perceived as a new teaching. A typical example is on the teaching on the indissolubility of marriage. When the people appealed to the writ of divorce allowed by the law of Moses, Jesus told them that it was not always like that at the beginning. But, that the concession was man made. He then explained how and why marriage was, and is, from the beginning indissoluble (Matt.19:3-9). Here, Jesus restores marriage to its original purity and fulfillment. The same practice can also be said of the institution of the Eucharist. Jesus instituted it within the context of the Jewish Passover meal. He did not change the matter of the celebration, rather, he gave a new form and meaning to the already existent matter (bread and wine) and feast. Judging from these practices, it is imperative that active agents of evangelization must avoid the imposition of practices that are neither essential to the goodnews nor could they be identified in the culture of the people. This subject will be discussed fully in the section on the Logic of Identity and Universality. For now, we will proceed to examine what John Paul II says about the new evangelization.

References

Chapter 3

1. Alphonso Cardinal Lo~pez Trujillo, "The Truth of the Human Being in Christ" in *Panorama*, pp.126-127.
2. John Paul II, "General Audience", December 13, 1978.
3. Schineller, *A Hand Book on Inculturation*, p.20.

4. Arrupe, "A Letter to the Whole Society", 13.

5. Teresa Okure, "Inculturation in the New Testament: Its Relevance for the Nigerian Church", in *Inculturation in Nigeria*, p.42.

6. Ibid., p.44.

7. Harve Carrier, "Inculturation: A Modern Approach to Evangelization", in *Inculturation in Nigeria*, p.11.

8. Schineller, *A Hand Book on Inculturation*, p.46.

9. John Paul II, Address to the University Community, Coimbra, Portugal, May 15, 1982.

10. Catechesi Tradendae, no.53.

11. Pope John Paul II, "Episcopal Ministry at the service of Life" (May 1980) in Africa: Apostolic Pilgrimage (Boston: Daughters of St. Paul, 1980), p.243.

12. The Nigerian Church: Evangelization through Inculturation, pp.13-14.

13. Ibid., p.14.

14. Ad Gentes, no.10.

15. Evangeli Nuntiandii, no.16.

16. Redemptor Hominis, no.1.

17. Redemptoris Missio, no.8.

18. Justin Ukpong, "Inculturation and Evangelization in New Testament Perspective," Paper presented at 3rd CIWA Theology Week Seminar, Port Harcourt, May 4, 1992, p.3.

19. The Lineamenta.

20. Ibid.,

21. John Paul II, "Homily", December 31, 1979.

22. Schineller, *A Hand book on Inculturation*, pp.61-63.

23. Peter Sarpong, "African Religion and Catholic Worship", A Talk given at the Eucharistic Congress in Philadelphia, August 1976, Cited by Schineller, *A Hand Book on Inculturation*, p.12.

24. Pope John Paul II, Address to the Nigerian Bishops. See *L'osservatore Romano*, February 24, 1982.

25. John Paul II, "African Bishops Challenge", in *African Address*, See also *Origins*, May 28, 1980, p.29.

26. Schineller, *A Hand Book on Inculturation*, p.21.

CHAPTER 4

POPE JOHN PAUL II ON THE NEW METHOD OF EVANGELIZATION

Evangelization is the proclamation of God's salvation to the ends of the earth. But since this had already been achieved by Christ by the incarnation event, the mission of evangelization today is to go out and proclaim and witness to the presence of Christ in the world. Inculturation is the new concept of evangelization which takes into consideration the whole history of salvation, beginning from creation through incarnation to the present-day evangelization mission. The whole concept is rooted on the missiological character of God's salvific activity.

The process by which God enters into human history, whether through creation or incarnation, is what is conceived by the Pope John Paul II as divine inculturation. The act of witnessing and the process by which the presence of Christ is witnessed as present in human culture is what is understood as inculturation in today's evangelization mission.

Pope John Paul II has been the author and great proponent of this new method and process of evangelization. Our purpose in this chapter therefore will be to examine what he says about the new method and how he effects this new method.

In the encyclical *Redemptoris Missio*, Pope John Paul II advocates for a way of proclaiming Christ to the world that is not antithetic to the other's freedom. In his own words he wrote: "Proclaiming Christ and bearing witness to him, when done in a way that respects consciences, does not violate freedom."*1* This proclamation, he says is to be made within the context of the individuals and people who receive it.*2* The question is, what is the *way* that the Pope is talking about? For him, there can be no other way than the way of inculturation wherein "proclaiming" and "witnessing" mean the announcement of the presence of Christ in the other or in a given culture. This is in keeping with the divine mandate "You shall be my witnesses" (Acts.1:8). To be a witness means to be part of, to be present at, and to give testimony of (or to) an event. Bearing witness to the faith therefore means, being there and announcing the presence of Christ *in* and *to* the other. Evangelization therefore becomes "the affirmation among peoples, of the gospel values which Jesus made incarnate in his own life (peace, justice, brotherhood, concern for the needy)."*3*

The Second Vatican Council Document *Gaudium et Spes* (GS) had anticipated this understanding of Christianity as being already sown in the minds and culture of the people by the incarnation event when it argued that incarnation effect:

> applies not only to Christian but to all people of good will in whose hearts grace is secretly at work. Since Christ died for everyone, and since the ultimate calling of each of us comes from God and is therefore a universal one, we are obliged to hold that the Holy Spirit offers everyone the possibility of sharing in this Paschal Mystery in a manner known to God.*4*

Christ himself, whose mission is the proclamation and establishment of God's kingdom (Lk 4:43), admits that the kingdom is already present on earth. Here one might note that the eschatological realism is not relegated to a remote "end of the world," but is already present, and at work in our midst (Mk. 1:15). God is revealed through that which is present. The kingdom aims at transforming human relationships; it grows gradually as people slowly learn to love, forgive and serve one another. By implication, anywhere there is love, forgiveness and service, there Christ is present. Pope John Paul II summed it up when he said:

> The kingdom's nature, therefore, is one of communion among all human beings with one another and with God. The kingdom is the concern of everyone: individuals, society, and the world. Working for the Kingdom means *acknowledging* and promoting Gods' activity, which is present in human history and transforms it. Building the Kingdom means working for liberation from evil in all its forms. In a word, the kingdom is the *manifestation* and the *realization* of God's plan of salvation in all its fullness.5

In another place he said:

> Missionary activity is nothing other and nothing less than the *manifestation* or *epiphany* of God's plan and its fulfillment in the world and in history, in this history God, by means of missions, clearly accomplishes the history of salvation. What paths does the church follow in order to achieve this goal?6

What could be observed from the quotations above is that in Pope John Paul II's definition of evangelization or proclamation of the kingdom, some key words like *witness*, *acknowledgement*, *manifestation* and *realization* become operative. These are the terms that help to link the relationship between evangelization, inculturation and incarnation.

Acknowledgement implies a recognition of something that is already there. We can only acknowledge an other. Manifestation entails a revelation of that which hitherto was present but hidden, it involves an unveiling. Realization has to do with a sudden awareness of something. Which ever way it is reasoned, for Pope John Paul II, evangelization has to do with the acknowledgement and proclamation of a divine presence which is already present through incarnation.

The use of the words manifestation or epiphany is very insightful. The missionary activity or evangelization is the manifestation (a making known or letting be seen) of God's plan of salvation. Just as Christ witnessed to the Father and proclaimed his kingdom on earth. "No one has at any time seen God" except "the only begotten son who is in the bosom of the father" (Jn.1:18, 14:7-14). Only he and he alone has revealed the Father. Like Christ, who bears witness to the Father, Christians are to bear witness to the presence of Christ and proclaim his presence. "You shall be my witnesses in Jerusalem and in all Judea and Samaria and to the ends of the earth" (Acts.1:8). John the Baptist bore witness and cried out:

> Behold the Lamb of God, who takes away the sin of the world. This is he of whom I said, "After me there comes one who has been set above me, because he was before me." And I did not know him. But that he may be known to Israel, for this reason have I come baptizing with water. (Jn.1:29-31)

God the Father bore witness to the son and proclaimed, "this is my beloved son in whom I am well pleased" (Matt.3:17).

In continuation with this tradition of witnessing, Pope John Paul II, while visiting with the Aborigines of Australia proclaimed the presence of God in their culture. He said:

> But for thousands of years you have lived in this land and
> fashioned a culture that endures to this day. And during all this
> time, the spirit of God has been with you. Your "Dreaming"
> which influences your lives so strongly that, no matter what
> happens, you remain forever people of your culture, is your
> own way of touching the mystery of God's spirit in you and in
> creation... through your closeness 7

Here the Pope returns to the original method of
evangelization, namely , witnessing to the presence of Christ.
Basing his vision on the decision of the First Church Council,
where it was agreed that it was, and is, not necessary for a
Gentile to submit to the Jewish law in order to become a
Christian. He championed the cause of inculturation in
evangelization. He urged the Aborigines to be Christian as
they are, within their culture. He exhorts evangelizers to take
into account peoples' hopes and expectations, their anguish
and sufferings as well as their culture, in order to proclaim to
them the goodnews. He cited the Speeches at Lystra and
Athens (Acts.14:15-1; 17:22-31) as models for
evangelization. 8 The Pope then showed how in these speeches
Paul enters into "dialogue" with the cultural and religious
values of different peoples. To the Lycaonians, who practiced
a cosmic religion, Paul speaks of religious experiences related
to the cosmos. With the Greeks, he discusses philosophy and
quotes their poets (Acts.17:18, 26-28). As the Pope noted:

> The God whom Paul wishes to reveal is already present in their
> lives, indeed, this God has created them and mysteriously guides
> nations and history ...' these are speeches which offer an
> example of the inculturation of the gospel. 9

Furthermore, quoting profusely from the scripture, Pope John
Paul II went on to show that the spirit of God is not limited in
its manifestation of God's presence. He wrote:

Thus the spirit who "blows where he wills" (Jn.3:8), who "was
already at work in the world before Christ was glorified" and
who "has filled the world ... holds all things together and knows
what is said" (Wis. 1:7), leads us to broaden our vision in order
to ponder his activity in every time and place. I have repeatedly
called this fact to mind and it has guided me in my meetings
with a wide variety of people.*10*

It must also be noted here that since the publication of the
Decree *Ad Gentes*, a line of theological reflection has
developed which emphasizes that the whole mystery of the
Church is contained in each particular church, provided it does
not isolate itself but remains in communion with the universal
Church and becomes missionary in its own turn.*11*
    It is this new line of theological reflection that allows for
the true universality of the Church. It is also this reflection that
allows us to see Christ as having incarnated in all cultures.
    Another interesting issue which Pope John Paul II
emphasizes is the issue of reciprocity in the evangelization
process. Respect for the particular church and respect for the
universal Church. In the same vein, respect for man in his
quest for answers to the deepest questions of his life and
respect for the action of the spirit in man.*12* One of the
insightful contributions of Pope John Paul II here is that for
him, every church is both particular and universal. The church
in Rome is as particular as it is universal and the church in
Poland is as universal as it is particular. Their relationship is
for the most part reciprocal. In every church there are
elements that reflect its universality and there are aspects that
pertain to its particularity.
    This notion of reciprocity is what the Pope discovered
in the dialogic relationship between creation and inculturation,
creation and incarnation; and incarnation and inculturation,

and incarnation and evangelization; and inculturation and evangelization.

Here Pope John Paul II recognizes the need for the dialogic relationship as being integral to inculturation and notes that it is through dialogue that the Church can uncover the "seeds of the Word", a "ray of truth which enlightens all people." This "seeds of the Word" and "ray of truth" he argues, are already found in individuals and in the religious traditions of humanity. This definitely is a type of dialogue that stimulates the Church to discover and acknowledge the signs of the presence and the workings of the Holy Spirit.*13*

Pope John Paul II's argument for the continuity of inculturation as it relates to creation, incarnation and the mission of the church is that it is the same spirit that was at work at creation that was and is at work in incarnation, and was at work at the Pentecost. He wrote:

> The same spirit who was at work in incarnation is at work in the church... whatever the spirit brings about in human hearts and in the history of peoples, in cultures and religions serve as a preparation for the gospel.14

Still arguing for inculturation as the matrix of the new evangelization process, he urges evangelizers to push forward to new frontiers and listen to the voice of the spirit. He said:

> Today the church must face other challenges and push forward to *new frontiers*, both in the initial mission *Ad_Gentes* and in the new evangelization of those peoples who have already heard Christ proclaimed. Today all Christians, the particular churches and the universal Church, are called to have the same courage that inspired the missionaries of the past, and the same readiness to listen to the voice of the spirit.*15*

The question is, what are these new frontiers directed toward both the initial mission and the new evangelization? There can be no other way of understanding the Pope's mind other than with reference to the central theme of the old evangelization strategy which he has rediscovered and named inculturation. For him, it is the solution to the 21st Century evangelization initiatives. It is the hope of the Third Millennium evangelization which the Pope has christened "evangelization 2000."

In the *Redemptoris Missio*, Pope John Paul II distinguishes three phases of evangelization.*16*

1) The first is the initial evangelization:

There is the situation which the Church's missionary activity addresses peoples, groups and socio-cultural contexts in which Christ and his Gospel are not known, or which lack Christian communities sufficiently mature to be able to incarnate the faith in their own environment and proclaim it to other groups. This is mission *Ad Gentes* in the initial sense of the term.

2) The Second is Pastoral Care:

There are Christian communities with adequate and solid ecclesiastical structures. they are fervent in their faith and in Christian living. they bear witness to the gospel in their surroundings and have a sense of commitment to the universal mission. In these communities the Church carries out her activity and pastoral care.

3) The Third is Re-evangelization:

There is an intermediate situation, particularly in countries with ancient Christian roots, and occasionally in younger churches as well, where entire groups of the Baptized have lost a living sense of the faith, or even no longer consider themselves members of the Church, and live a life far removed from Christ and his gospel. In this case what is needed is a new "evangelization" or a "re-evangelization."

What is new in this three staged project of evangelization is that in all these phases, inculturation according to Pope John Paul II, is the only approach that can help make the goodnews meaningful and relevant to the people. What is more, these three phases can be likened to the Trinitarian process or the three stages of salvation history. The similitude could be represented summarily as follows:

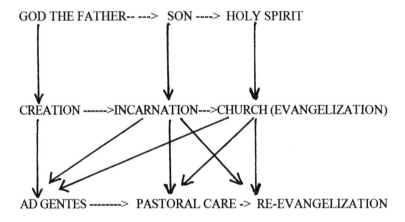

God the Father through creation reaches out to the ends of the earth. God the son (by incarnation) brings the goodnews from the Father to the ends of the earth, cares for believers and re-evangelizes a defaulted human nature. Incarnation thus redeems creation and continues the work of redemption through the church. God the Holy Spirit through the Church carries out the mission of God the Father and God the Son to the ends of the earth, cares and strengthens believers and re-evangelizes the weak. The Church (all Christians and ministers) continue the mission of the Father, the Son and the Holy Spirit.

The horizontal relationship shows both the incarnational and the inculturational mission while the downward motion relationship shows both the inculturational and the evangelizational mission. However, knowing how inculturation and evangelization are related in the Father - Son - Holy Spirit relationship; and in the Creation - Incarnation - Church relationship, one must admit that the attempted distinctions are very tenuous. The relationships are much richer and mutually complementing than what appears to be presented. As Pope John Paul II himself admits, "the boundary between Pastoral care of the faithful, new evangelization and specific missionary activity are not clearly definable, and it is unthinkable to create barriers between them or put into watertight compartments."*17*

On the specifics, of how the various phases are to be achieved, in addition to the general mission *Ad Gentes*, he recommends liturgical inculturation for the achievement of pastoral care. On the re-evangelization mission, he notes that attention should be focused on the new cultural forms that are imaging in the modern world. He said:

> Today the image of mission *Ad Gentes* is perhaps changing: efforts should be concentrated on the big cities, where new customs and styles of living arise together with new forms of culture and communication.*18*

Here Pope John Paul II alludes to the possibility of inculturation even among the people who had been evangelized but now their way of life has assumed a new cultural orientation. Can the goodnews still be preached to them in this new cultural attire? The Pope believes that it is possible through inculturation. This is what he meant by "new evangelization" when he addressed the American Bishops in these words:

> But how is the American culture evolving today? Is this evolution being influenced by the Gospel? Does it clearly reflect Christian inspiration? Your music, your poetry and art, your drama, your painting and scripture, the literature that you are producing - are those things which reflect the soul of a nation being influenced by the spirit of Christ for the perfection of humanity.[19]

What Pope John Paul II has in mind here is the possibility of evangelizing the culture as a means of redeeming the totality of man including his environment. If the human culture is christified or evangelized, then man himself will be redeemed.

It is this mission of re-evangelization through culture that brings the Pope to the American nation as often as he is opportuned. He believes that the American nation as well as other European nations whose culture he has described on many occasions as the "culture of death" needs to be re-evangelized. On how this is to be done, he cited the example of the value of the mass media culture. He said:

> Involvement in the mass media, however is not meant merely to strengthen the preaching of the gospel. There is a deeper reality involved here: since the very evangelization of modern culture depends to a great extent on the influence of the media, it is not enough to use the media simply to spread the Christian message and the church's authentic teaching. It is also necessary to integrate that message into the "new culture" created by modern communication.[20]

The questions that one might want to ask here are: What is the "deeper reality" in the involvement of the mass media in evangelization? What does Pope John Paul II intend in the claim that it is necessary to integrate the message into the "new culture"? There is no doubt that the deeper reality in question and the process of integration could be found in what Pope John Paul II has identified as inculturation. Can the goodnews be seen to, in any way, be emanating in the new culture? This is a question which only inculturation can answer.

On the process of the practice of inculturation for evangelizers, the Pope maintains that evangelizers must move beyond their present cultural limitation and immerse themselves in the cultural milieu of those they intend to evangelize. To achieve this, they must learn the language of the place in which they work, become familiar with the most important expressions of the culture. This he says is to enable the evangelizers discover the new values through direct experience.21 It is only if they have this kind of awareness he says, will they be able to bring to the people the knowledge of the "hidden mystery."

What John Paul II is prescribing here is in imitation of Christ who moved beyond his divine (heavenly culture) and immersed himself in human culture, learnt the human language, became familiar with the most important expressions of the Jewish culture which was in the Passover celebration and through it he brought to the people the hidden mystery of God's salvation. For Pope John Paul II, it is only through this kind of immersion for the purpose of understanding, appreciating, fostering and evangelizing the culture that solidarity can be achieved with the people. This solidarity will be the ultimate end of inculturation. Just as through incarnation Christ was and is able to become "one with man in all things but sin," through inculturation (evangelization) solidarity, oneness will be achieved among Christians. Eventually, the ultimate solidarity between God and the created order will be achieved when all things would have been restored to God through Christ. This notion of solidarity is a very important theme in the thought of John Paul II.

The summary of what has been discussed here is that inculturation accompanies the whole of the missionary life. As Pope John Paul II notes, it is "a slow journey which accompanies the whole of the missionary life."22 The missionary life begins with creation, incarnation and evangelization. Just as inculturation is the underlying process in creation, incarnation and evangelization, it is also involved in the three phases of evangelization: Initial evangelization, Pastoral Care and Re-evangelization.

References

Chapter 4

1. *Redemptoris Missio*, no.8.
2. Ibid., no.44.
3. Ibid., no.3.
4. *Gaudium et Spes*, no.22.
5. *Redemtoris Missio*, no.15.
6. Ibid., no.41.

7. Pope John Paul II, Address to the People of Australia, November 29, 1986. Cited by Joseph Cardinal Cordeiro, "The Religious Sense of Man", in *Panorama,* p.71.

8. *Redemptoris Missio,* no.25.

9. Ibid.,

10. Ibid., no.29.

11. Ibid., no.48. See also the Decree on the Missionary Activity of the Church *Ad Gentes*, Ch. III.

12. John Paul II, Address to Representatives of Non-Christian Religions, Madras, February 5, 1986. See also Message to the Peoples of Asia, Manila, Feb.21, 198.

13. *Redemptoris Missio,* no.56.

14. Ibid., no.29.

15. Ibid., no.30.

16. Ibid., no.33.

17. Ibid., no.34.

18. Ibid., no.37.

19. Pope John Paul II, Address to the U.S. Catholic Bishops at Queen of the Angels Minor Seminary, Los Angeles, September 16 1987; See John Paul II in America, St. Paul Books and Media, 1987, p.198.

20. Redemptoris Missio, no. 37.

21. Ibid., no.53.

22. Ibid., no.52.

CHAPTER 5

POPE JOHN PAUL II: A Symbol of Inculturation

It is a truism that actions speak louder than words. It is also true that actions and signs are effective and personalized tools of communication. For example, if the lady of the house coughs at the dinner table, her dinner guests may think that she has a cold or is choked. But her child, sitting at the foot of the table, knows right away that this is her mothers signal to him that he has picked up the wrong fork. His mother means everything to him, and so the child seeks in her eyes what others have been combing books to find.*1*

Pope John Paul II has spoken and written so much about inculturation. Many have searched for the meaning of what he means by inculturation in books, but this text looks and finds in the person and actions of Pope John Paul II, the true meaning and practice of inculturation. As he himself explained in his encyclical *Redemptoris Missio*, since the "goodnews" is Christ, there is an identity between the message and the messenger, between saying, doing and being. Christ's evangelization power and the secret of the effectiveness of his actions, lie in his total identification with the message he announces. With a similar approach, Pope John Paul II in his sayings, actions and person seeks to be the symbol and presence of inculturation. As noted by Jan Cardinal Willebrands, President of the Secretariat for the Unity of Christians, the Pope's actions "have been and are in harmony with his teaching, a practical catechesis and a gift offered to all."2 Bishop John R. Roach shared the same view of the Pope when he noted that "it is impossible to separate the person of Pope John Paul II from his actions and teachings".3 Our task, therefore, in this chapter will be to examine the person and actions of Pope John Paul II with the hope of showing how they are symbols of inculturation.

John Paul II's election as Pope was and is symbolic. *"Annuntio Vobis_Gaudium Magnum: Habemus Papam!"* These were the words of Cardinal Felici, the Dean of the College of Cardinals when he announced the election of Pope John Paul II on October 16, 1978. "I announce to you a great joy: we have a Pope, the most eminent and most Reverend Lord, Cardinal of the Holy Roman Church, Karol Wojtyla, who has taken the name, John Paul II."

Like the emergence of a new creation, out of an existing stuff, there emerged from the Sistine a Pope who was a non-Italian. Something new had happened, the curtain had been raised, and the veil of ignorance, as it were, had been removed. Inculturation had taken place on the chair of Peter. The Holy Spirit had seen and loved in Karol Wojtyla, a Pole, what for Centuries he had seen and loved in Italians. The choice of a non-Italian as the Vicar of Christ ushered in a new era. This had not happened since the Pontificate of Adrian VI (1522 - 1523), who was a Dutchman.

October 16, 1978 was a day of reliving the original practice of the Church, wherein Peter, a non-Roman could become the first Bishop of Rome - Pope. Pope John Paul II emerged, and the crowds at St. Peter's square were stunned. As an eye witness account reported, "the crowd behind the police barriers in the square did not know what to do; people's curled index fingers furtively wiped the lower lids of their obviously misty eyes."4 Could they believe their eyes? Like the story of the election of David (1 Sam. 16), it was not any of the more known Cardinals that they saw. It was not any of the well known names that they heard. They saw the face and heard the name that was unfamiliar to their eyes and strange to their ears - Karol Wojtyla.

Customarily, it was not the case, that a new Pope should address the people on the occasion of the announcement of his election. But John Paul II, to the amazement of the Prefects of protocol, broke with custom and tradition and spoke to the people. Perhaps, having seen how the crowds were bewildered at the announcement of his election, he needed to reassure them.

The new Pope, solemnly, and in the words of the divine master addressed the people. "Do not be afraid." Like Christ speaking to the Apostles during the stormy sea, he calmed the troubled minds. The square was dead silent. Everybody wanting to hear what the "unusual" Pope had to say. And since then, the whole world has been yearning and listening to what the Pope from Poland has to say. Pope John Paul II himself has been unrelenting in carrying his message to the ends of the earth, whether it is to the United Nations Assembly or to the remotest part of the world.

But, his first address, "Do not be afraid," has become the subject of great discourse among both his admirers and critics alike. Do not be afraid; of what? One can only conjecture what was in the mind of Karol Wojtyla when he addressed the people. "Do not be afraid perhaps to accept the will of God and the power of the Holy Spirit. The same power that made it possible for God to become man, for a virgin to conceive, has transformed me and made me Pope." The rest of what the Pope might have intended in the statement has been documented in his new book, *Beyond the Threshold of Hope.5*

What did it signify, that Karol Wojtyla had been made Pope? What could be said here is that, for a non-Italian to become Pope, was a sign that the Holy Spirit was returning to the beginnings, for the purpose of further universalizing the "goodnews". After all, Peter, the first Supreme Pontiff was never an Italian. So, with the election of Karol Wojtyla as Pope, inculturation had taken place even with the papacy. And, as observed by Joseph Cardinal Bernadine, the Archbishop of Chicago, "being the only Polish Pope in the Church's history, he brings a distinctive perspective to his role as 'the visible source and foundation of unity' of the Church."6

Like his immediate predecessor, he broke with tradition and took the name John Paul II. But this "breakage" and "return" was hermeneutical in that it constituted a certain type of continuity. The name John Paul symbolized a promise and a heritage of Pope John XXIII and the hope of Pope Paul VI. At the same time the name John Paul also signified a return to the origins. John, for John the Evangelist and the Incarnation theologian. John the Evangelist in his gospel wrote:

> In the beginning was the word, and the word was with God; and the word was God. All things were made through him and without him was made nothing that has been made ... and the word was made flesh, and dwelt among us... (Jn.1:1-18).

Here John the Evangelist proclaims the incarnation theology. A theological thought that has remained the center stage and the fountain head of Pope John Paul II's thought.

The name Paul signifies his heritage of Paul the Apostle and missionary apostle *Ad Gentes*. Thus, in Pope John Paul II, we see on the one hand, the continuity of John the Evangelist and Paul the Apostle, and on the other, the heritage of Pope John XXIII and that of Pope Paul VI.

Pope John Paul II's crowning ceremony was also symbolic. Unlike his Italian predecessors, the non-Italian Pope had no need of a crown. And so, he demanded that he be crowned without a crown. Instead of a crown, he wore a Miter.7 This again was a break with the established tradition. What shall we say, emanation of new cultural behavior from within the papacy. This was inculturation in action.

Another symbolic act about John Paul II is his travels. He was elected on October 16, 1978, but by the end of the following January he was already in Puebla, Mexico. Since then, he has travelled more than 600,000 miles (twice the distance between the earth and the moon) to announce the gospel. He has made 68 trips outside Italy and has visited 148 countries of the world.8 The latest travel which is not numbered among the 148 trips is his recent visit to the Republic of Germany. These travels typify the apostolic method of missionary journey. Pope John Paul II has expanded it to planetary dimension. On his arrival in Mexico, he explained his mission thus: "The Lord and master of history and of our destinies, has wished my pontificate to be that of a pilgrim pope of evangelization, working down the roads of the world, bringing to all peoples the message of salvation."9

As the successor of Peter he stays in Rome but as Paul he goes on missionary work. He admitted to the purpose of his journeys in his encyclical *Redemptoris Missio* when he said: "From the beginning of my Pontificate I have chosen to travel to the ends of the earth in order to show this missionary concern."*10* Here the Pope admits that the purpose of his travels is to bring the goodnews to the ends of the earth. In his Sermon at Aqueduct New York (Oct. 6, 1995) he said this of himself: " The Pope's presence (and Address at the 50th anniversary of the United Nations Organization) at that international forum is an act of evangelization, aimed at serving the progress of humanity in the great family of nations ...." For the Pope, his very presence at the Assembly has an evangelizing effect.

Pope John Paul II is definitely conscious of Christianity as a religion of *Presence*. Its (Christianity) revelation is the revealing of a presence of God. The incarnation is a presence, the Eucharist is a presence. Thus the Pope's mission is to be present to the world. He goes out to see and witness to the presence of Christ in the world and to make him more present in and to the world.

As Pope John Paul II affirmed in the opening section of his first encyclical *Redemptor Hominis*, Jesus Christ is the center of the universe and of history. He believes this with conviction in the tradition of all Pontiffs. Surely, the message of Pope John Paul II has a different emphasis from that of his recent predecessors but is still in keeping with the tradition of the apostolic missionaries. Such gestures as kissing the ground in all the countries that he visits, does betray a difference in emphasis but is definitely a return to the Pauline practice of respect for the "unknown God" (Acts.17:22-34). Because he believes that Christ is the center of the universe and history, he recognizes the divine presence and activity in other cultures. He believes in the fulfillment of the incarnation event. His love of and respect for what is other is significant. Thus his travels are for the purpose of giving witness to the presence of Christ in the world. It is for this reason that he effects a liturgical inculturation in every   country where he visits, by celebrating mass with a chasuble made of the local fabric and often embroidered with local symbols and insignia.

Josef Cardinal Tomko, the Prefect of the Congregation for the Evangelization of Peoples, has offered an insightful reading of the significance of the Pope's travels when he says:

> The Pope clearly understands that "mission" means the revelation of God's power for salvation of whoever believes. It is in the context of the urgency of this manifestation that all and everyone of the journeys and pilgrimages of the Pope assumes their full significance. The journeys are visits paid to each of the local churches, and demonstrate the place that these communities have in the universal dimensions of the church, and underline the particular role they play in the building up of the church's universality.11

It is interesting that Tomko describes the Pope's travels as pilgrimages. A pilgrimage is a visit to a holy place or a place of significant religious importance. So the places that the Pope visits are already holy places wherein he goes to confirm or reaffirm their holiness. Pope John Paul II himself confirmed this insight when he admitted that every trip of his is a "a genuine pilgrimage to the living sanctuary of the People of God."12 Because of this conviction, anywhere the Pope goes, he shows appreciation of the religious spirit that exists in the different cultural traditions. For example, while in Japan, He said:

> You are the heirs and the keepers of an ancient wisdom. The wisdom in Japan and in the Orient has inspired high degrees of moral life. It has taught you to venerate the pure, transparent and honest heart. It has inspired you to discover

the divine presence in every creature, and especially in every human being.*13*

Here the Pope, like Paul in Athens, sees what is good in the Japanese culture. Thus, taking the message to the ends of the earth, he finds in other places, what he sees, perceives and loves both in Poland and in Rome.

One of the uncanny characteristics of Pope John Paul II is his fidelity to and continuity of the Council's traditions, the Fathers of the Church and the Scripture. As noted by Frossard:

> Whenever he has to work out a doctrinal matter, he conforms his explanations to the teachings of the Church Fathers, and at every stage he makes certain that his words are consistent with what is laid down in Holy Scripture, so that he can use both these sources as pitons.*14*

Another example of his fidelity and commitment, similar to that noted above, is his insistence on inculturation as the matrix and foundation of evangelization. He knows that the practice is as old as Christianity itself. Having drawn from the experience of the apostolic times, through the first great missions of the Church into the outer reaches of the Roman Empire, there is no doubt in his mind that the Church, ancient and present regards inculturation as her traditional method of fulfilling her missionary vocation to the peoples and cultures of the world. He comes, therefore, to this practice with a renewed enthusiasm and understanding that relives the old practice creatively. His hermeneutical return to the roots is reminiscent of mountain trails that sometimes must descend in order to reach the safest place to begin climbing again.

It might be of interest to note here that even in the domestic affairs of the Vatican court, the presence of the Pope

John Paul II, occasions a form of domestic inculturation. Inculturation in the papacy takes root from the kitchen to the sanctuary of St. Peter's square. In the kitchen, it is Polish sisters (Srs. Fernand, Mathilde, Eufrosyna, Tobiana and Germana) of the Congregation of the Sacred Heart of Jesus who ensure that there is a Polish touch to what the Pope eats. And since we are and become what we eat, even in Rome, the Pope still remains Polish. Polish nuns prepare the Holy Fathers meals and members of the same Polish Order manage the Papal household.*15* At Christmas, the Pope sings Polish carols with the Polish household at the Vatican. As Tad Szulc has noted: "You can take the Pope out of Poland but you cannot take Poland out of the Pope."*16* Just as Christ is truly human and truly divine, John Paul II is truly Pope as he is truly Polish. That is what inculturation has achieved. The unity of the particular church with the universal Church in the person of Pope John Paul II.

One other aspect of Pope John Paul II's inculturative enterprise is noticeable in the intellectual content of his encyclicals. The encyclicals are strongly rooted in his Polish experience. His theological and philosophical framework is a carry over of the Lublin/Cracow School of thought.*17* For example, his book, *Sources of Renewal* (1972), appears to have been an application of the phenomenological conclusions of the Lublin/Cracow School to difficult topics of Faith, such as Church. In this text he showed how the Church begins with God and moving towards man (incarnation) on the one hand and on the other, with man and moving towards God (evangelization). The unity being achieved in God becoming man and man becoming divine through Christ. It is this process of becoming, that Pope John Paul II was to describe as inculturation in his later writings as Pope. It was this insight that Pope John Paul II, then the

Cardinal Archbishop of Cracow, had in mind at the publication of his *Sources of Renewal* (1972). In this text too, he told the Polish people that many had missed the point of the Second Vatican Council on Renewal. He patiently explained in the text what he believed was the teaching of the Council on renewal. When eventually he became Pope, he passed the same message to the world. And today, we have come to understand that for Pope John Paul II the major sources and process of renewal in the Church are: Incarnation - (Inculturation) - and evangelization.

What is evident in the thought of Pope John Paul II is that he has brought the phenomenological realism of the Cracow School to bear in his analysis of Christian doctrine. It is this heritage that has enabled him to evolve a new concept and perception of incarnation and evangelization within the matrix and rubrics of a new procedural phenomenon called inculturation.

On the Pope's indebtedness to his family tradition, there is a story about him when he was twelve years old. He was a member of the church choir but noted to have been disinterested in choir practices. His father who was a disciplinarian said to him one day, "'you are not being a very good choir boy. You do not pray to the Holy Spirit enough. You ought to pray to him.' His father taught him a prayer to the Holy Spirit."*18*

In writing the encyclical, *Dominum et Vivificantem* on the Holy Spirit, John Paul II admits that it was the prayer that his father taught him, that influenced the writing and the theme of this encyclical. The Pope says this of his father:

> He taught me a prayer to say ... that was a major spiritual lesson, longer-lasting and more powerful than anything I got from my reading or from the courses I took later on. What conviction his voice held as he told me that, I can still hear his voice saying

those words, even today. The end-product of that lesson from my
childhood is my encyclical on the Holy Spirit.*19*

This admission of Pope John Paul II is not only revealing but
instructive. Even an encyclical written for the universal
church has its roots and sources from a bedroom counsel
between father and son in a small town in Poland. What does
this say about our understanding of the source of universality
in the church? Surely one could say that it is the particular
that makes the universal.

Pope John Paul II's acts do not only break with
tradition for the purpose of expanding the kingdom, but, he
often does this within the context of who he is, a Pope who
is also a Pole. Pope John Paul II came to Rome as Pope with
polish experience. As the Latin expression says: *Quid quid
recipitur ad modum recipientis_recipitur.* What ever is
received is received according to the mode of the receiver. So
it was, and is, with the Pope. For example, in his experience,
the most immediate act of charity or heroic act that was most
present to him was that of Maximilian Kolbe. Maximilian
Kolbe was a polish Franciscan. While he (Maximilian) was in
the concentration camp during the Gestapo regime (1940) he
freely offered to trade places with a father of a family who
was to be executed. His acceptance to die for another, was
seen as a heroic act. When it came to canonizing the first
Saint of his pontificate, it was Maximilian that the Pope first
remembered.

With Maximilian's canonization (Oct.1979), Pope John
Paul II occasioned a redefinition of what it takes to be a
martyr. According to tradition, a martyr was defined as "one
who testifies to the Faith, even unto death inflicted as an act
of hatred of the Faith." One of the consultants on the
definition of martyrdom explained that since Faith is bound

up with love, and an act of charity is also an act of faith, it was reasonable that Maximilian be canonized for his act of love. Thus, with this new definition, Pope John Paul II saw in his country-man what other Popes saw in Saints. What is more, with the canonization of Maximilian, a tradition was broken, inculturation (emergence of a new cultural form from within an existent one) which enlivens the old and the new, was achieved.

Inculturation in a sense entails a break with tradition. But as already mentioned, it is a type of break that in effect, perfects and continues the tradition in a new light. Pope John Paul II, both in his person and activity has epitomized this process. Because his evangelization thrust is for all, he ventures into the hitherto "no go" areas.

He is the first Pope to visit the Italian President in his court. Like God who had no shame in becoming man so as to save man, Pope John Paul is not afraid or ashamed to leave his sanctuary in Rome to the Italian presidency if only that will help in evangelizing the Italian politicians.

He is the first Pope to ever visit a Synagogue. Apart from Christ and St. Peter, the first Pontiff, no other Catholic Pontiff had or has ever visited a synagogue. But Pope John Paul II has done it. He saw in the synagogue what Christ saw when he went in and unrolled the Scroll to proclaim the word to the people, to bring the goodnews to the Jews, to evangelize and to engage in a type of ecumenical discourse (Lk. 4:16-18). What ever was the content of the discussion between the Pope and the Rabbi is not the subject at issue here. The fact that the Pope visited the synagogue is symbolic enough for our purpose. All that the Pope wanted to achieve as he later admitted was to show by his presence that the Church recognizes in Israel the elder brother of Christian people in the order of revelation.20 Like Christ and Peter, who were not afraid of the synagogue, Pope John Paul II relived the old practice in a new way.

For Pope John Paul II, the missionary thrust belongs to the very nature of the Christian life, and is also the inspiration behind ecumenism: "that they may all be one ... so that the world may believe that you have sent me" (Jn.17:21). On November 30, 1979, he took part in the eucharistic liturgy in the church of Saint George at the ecumenical Patriarchate. On May 29, 1982 he prayed together with the Primate of the Anglican Communion at Canterbury Cathedral. During the visit of Patriarch Dimitrios I on December 6, 1987 to the Vatican, Pope John Paul II held a service with the Patriarch. On October 5, 1991, he joined the Lutheran Archbishops, the Primates of Sweden and Finland for the celebration of vespers at St. Peters Basilica on the occasion of the 6th Centenary of the canonization of Saint Birgitta. Surely, the ecumenical endeavors of Pope John Paul II does give a new character to the catholicity of the Church.

Apart from these ecumenical moves, there is something else that Pope John Paul II has done which does not only reflect the universal character of the Church but is a calculated effort to achieve what could be described here as "a diversity in unity." As Christians and Catholics, we are all, already united in Christ. Pope John Paul II seeks to foster this unity by his emphasis on the diversity of cultures as a reflection of the many faces of Christ. This is very noticeable in his appointment of Prefects and Heads of Congregations.

It might be of interest to note here, that since the early history of the Church, when Victor I (189 - 199), Miltiades (312 - 313), and Gelasius (492 - 499), all Africans, were elected Popes, no other African has held a highest ranking position in the Vatican Congregation till the pontificate of Pope John Paul II. In 1984, Pope John Paul II appointed

Bernadin Cardinal Gantin, from one of the smallest countries of West Africa, Republic of Benin, as Head of the most powerful organ of government in the Universal Church - the Prefect of the Congregation of Bishops. Cardinal Gantin works closely with the Pope, helping him to decide who is to be named bishop or cardinal. He is also the Dean of the College of Cardinals.

Prior to Pope John Paul II, the emphasis was on "unity in diversity," wherein all efforts were geared towards bringing all the people who hitherto did not belong, to be part at least peripherally, of the universal Church as already defined. Thus forcing a unity or more appropriately "a marriage of convenience." But with inculturation as the guide, Pope John Paul II seeks after and achieves a new dimension, namely, "diversity in unity." The understanding is that all are already united in Christ and therefore he seeks to build and strengthen the unity by emphasizing the diversity that highlights the union. Here, it is the people together in their diversity that defines the universality of the Church. A look at the list of the Prefects of the Congregations and Heads of Councils reveals the new character of the church - the Church universal and united. This is what the list shows:

Successor of Peter ----- Pope John Paul II (Poland).

Prefect, Congregation for bishops --
Bernadin cardinal Gantin (Benin).

Prefect, Congregation for the Doctrine of Faith --
Joseph Cardinal Ratzinger (Germany).

Prefect, Congregation for the Propagation of the Faith --
Joseph Cardinal Tomko (Slovakia)

Head, Council for Promoting of Christian Unity --

Edward Cardinal Cassidy (Australia).

President, Council for the Laity --
Eduardo Cardinal Pironio (Argentina).

Head, Council for Justice and Peace --
Roger Cardinal Etchegaray (France).

Head, Pontifical Council for Social Communication --
Archbishop John Foley (America).

Head, Council for the Family --
Alfonso Cardinal Lopez Trujillo (Colombia).

Head, Council for Inter - Religious Dialogue --
Francis Cardinal Arinze (Nigeria).

With this different nationalities and cultures blending together to epitomize the universal Church in Rome, one cannot but experience the extent to which inculturation is effected in the Church. Inculturation has really taken place in the Church and thus bringing out the best of what it means to be Universal and Catholic. All this is owed for the most part to the vision of inculturation envisioned by Pope John Paul II. By his approach, he is truly seeking to return the Church to its original purity, where being a gentile or a Jew was not an issue but having faith in Christ was the only requirement.

When the Pope visited his home country, he was not bashful in showing that the Pope was Polish and that the Polish church was universal. As observed by Tad Szulc:

John Paul II is the Pontiff of the universal church, a key player on the world diplomatic scene, but remains a polish patriot, a polish philosopher, a polish theologian, a polish poet, and a polish politician. During his first Papal visit to Poland in June 1979, the embroidered insignia on his chasuble - the Orphrey - was the polish royal crowned white eagle with gold letters on blue proclaiming *Polonai Semper Fidelis* (Poland Always Faithful)... *21*

Based on John Paul II's words and actions Tad Szulc further commented: "You can take the Pope out of Poland but you cannot take Poland out of the Pope."*22* Pope John Paul II, the Pope from Poland is at the same time the symbol of the universal Church.

Another very noticeable contribution of Pope John Paul II to the task of inculturation in the life of the Church is in the area sainthood. A recent report by an Italian Newspaper, *La Stampa*, noted that Pope John Paul II has raised more people toward sainthood than all of his 20th Century predecessors. Even some very eminent Cardinals in Rome have openly criticized the pontiff for enlarging the holy pantheon of Saints to include those from other cultures. In a recent Memoirs published by Sivio Cardinal Oddi, a 85 year old veteran of the Vatican administration, he chided the Vatican for having "become a saint factory." This comment was an open disapproval of the current practice of encouraging the beatification and canonization of some notably holy men and women from the local churches.

Pope John Paul II is right in his approach. There is inculturation in sainthood. After all, did the Ugandan youths (St. Charles Lwanga and companions) not die as martyrs? For that, they were canonized saints for the universal Church. St Augustine of Hippo, one of the most eminent saints in the history of the Church was a Barber from Tagaste in North Africa. Surely, there must be more saints in heaven than can ever be numbered by the human mind.

Pope John Paul II is consistent in his mission. His emphasis on beatification and canonization of saints especially in the developing world seems to be necessitated by the need to give the Catholics of diverse cultures local models of virtue. This is a welcome development, it surely brings the Church closer to the people. The practice is a new form of evangelization. It is certainly inculturation in action.

Finally, let us admit that Pope John Paul II is a man with a difference. He means every word of what he says and does. When he told the American church that "it is necessary to integrate the message of the gospel into the new culture created by modern communication," he meant every word of it. Perhaps if Christ were born today, he would show himself on the internet -- the information highway. And so, on the 25th of December 1995 (Christmas Day), Pope John Paul II authorized access to the Vatican through the internet. What does this say about the missionary Church?

This event cannot be perceived outside of the person of Pope John Paul II. The itinerant and missionary Pope, having realized, that on account of age and physical inability, he may no longer be in a position to undertake personal travels to the ends of the world, searched for new ways by which he can reach the world without leaving Rome. He found the solution in the new culture of the technology of information sharing called internet. It is easy, just enter this code http://www.vatican.va and you will be on line with the Vatican.

Pope John Paul II, by authorizing the Vatican to be accessed through the internet, has effected a new mode of evangelization. As Joaquin Navarro-Valls, the Papal spokesman on communication matters said, "the people now have direct contact with him (Pope) and the Church, and it helps us fulfill the mission of preaching the gospel." Similarly, Sister Judith Zoebelein, who herself is one of the architects of this new initiative admitted that "there's enormous potential for new evangelization" with the internet. What then shall we say?

Surely, this event is a marriage of the old Church with the new technology (culture). After all, Christ in his triumphant entry to Jerusalem used the donkey which was the most available means of transportation of His time. So Pope John Paul is right in using the most available means of communication to spread the goodnews. This, definitely, is a new dimension of inculturation. A new way of perceiving how the goodnews is to be communicated has emanated. By this singular act, the Pope John Paul II has revolutionized the evangelization process.

Inculturation we have defined as the act and process by which a new cultural form emanates from or is perceived in an already existing one. What else can we ask for in Pope John Paul II? In him we see the universal Church incarnate and the local church universalized. In him we see the missionary Church. There are, definitely, new forms that have emanated from or can be perceived in the Church of Christ that has always existed and has always been missionary. In the language of Pedro Arrupe, in John Paul II we see the Christian message not only finding expression through the elements proper to the polish culture but becomes the factor that animates, directs and unifies the Church, transforming it into a new creation. To use the language of John Paul II himself, in the Pope from Poland, we see the "incarnation of the gospel (goodnews) in an autochthonous culture" (the polish culture). We also see in him the "introduction of this (polish) culture into the life of the church", to the point that it produces a pope for the universal Church.

Pope John Paul II is really, both in his person and in his actions, a symbol of inculturation.

References

Chapter 5

1. See Andre~ Frossard, *Portraite of John Paul II*, (San Francisco: Ignatius Press, 1990), p.48.

2. Jan Cardinal Willebrands, "John Paul II and the search for full Unity among Christians" in *Panorama*, p.53.

3. John R. Roach, "Foreword" in *Covenant of Love*, by R. M. Hogan and J.M. LeVoir, (San Francisco: Ignatius Press, 1992), p.9.

4. Portraite of John Paul II, p.16.

5. John Paul II, *Crossing the Threshold of Hope*, (New York: Alfred A. Knopf, 1994), pp.218-224.

6. Joseph Cardinal Bernadine, "Preface" in *Panorama*, p.7.

7. Portraite of John Paul II, p.16.

8. See *Inside the Vatican* (Special Issue), Year 3, #10, November 1995 p.30.

9. Pope John Paul II, Arrival Speech in Mexico city, May 6, 1990; *L'Osservatore Romano* (English Edition) May 7, 1990, pp.1, 12.

10. Redemptoris Missio, no.1.

11. Josef Cardinal Tomko, "Mission and Dialogue in the Teaching of John Paul II" in *Panorama*, p.92.

12. John Paul II, *Insegnamenti*, II, p.765.

13. Address to the Church in Tokyo, (1981). Cited by Joseph Cardinal Cordeiro, in *Panorama*, p.70.

14. Portraite of John Paul II, p.70.

15. Inside Vatican, "Photo essay" by Crista Kramer, November 1995, p.1V.

16. Tad Szulc, *John Paul II: The Biography*, (New York: NY, Scribner, 1995), p.24.

17. For a detailed study of his indebtedness to the Lublin/Cracow School, See *Covenant of Love,* pp.29-33. See also Ludvik Nemec, *Pope John Paul II: A Festive Profile* (New York: Catholic Book Publishing, 1979) ch.8,10,15.

18. This story was narrated by Pope John Paul II himself to Andre~ Frossard, a close friend of the Pope. See *Portraite_of John Paul II,* p.74.

19. Ibid., p.74.

20. For details of the visit, See *Portraite of John Paul II,* p.97.

21. Tad Szulc, *John Paul II: The Biography,* p.24.

22. Ibid.

CHAPTER 6

HERMENEUTICS AND INCULTURATION

The purpose of this chapter is to show that hermeneutics is the most rational foil for understanding inculturation. For example, the notion of reciprocity in the inculturation process which John Paul II has argued for cannot be fully appreciated unless it is reasoned and understood within the dialectics of hermeneutical return. We shall therefore begin this chapter by examining what hermeneutics is and later show how inculturation is hermeneutical.

6.1 What is Hermeneutics?

According to Frederick Nietzsche, "all concepts in which an entire process is semeiotically concentrated, elude definitions."1 Hermeneutics is one of such terms. It is rather difficult to find a single predication that would serve as a sufficient explanation of what hermeneutics is. However, for the purpose of our discourse, we shall try to examine the meaning of the term via its root origin.

The etymology of the term hermeneutics is rooted in Hermes, the messenger of the gods of the ancient religious traditions of both the Egyptians and the Greeks. As the messenger and interpreter of the messages of the gods, Hermes had to be conversant with the idioms of the gods as well as that of the humans. He had to understand and interpret for himself what the gods wanted to convey before he could proceed to translate and explain the intention of the gods to humans. It is this Hermes' task of having to go forward and backward (from the gods to humans and from humans to the gods) both in understanding and interpretation that is often referred to as the hermeneutical journey.

Drawing from its root meaning scholars developed special rules of interpretation regarding written texts especially the biblical texts. Thus the art of interpreting the bible by imagining and returning to the original context of discourse came to be understood as hermeneutics.

But in the 19th Century, two German Scholars Frederick Schleiermacher and William Dilthey succeeded in transforming hermeneutics from the study and collection of specialized rules of interpretation for the use of theologians to that of a genuine philosophical discipline and general theory of the social and human sciences. Schleiermacher viewed hermeneutics as the art of understanding while Dilthey maintained that hermeneutics is both the art and science of understanding and interpretation. The philosophical problem that ensued centered on the question of whether we have to understand in other to interpret or whether we have to interpret in other to understand. There has been so much debate on this subject as scholars continue to search for ways of either understanding or interpreting reality. Some have defended the position that all forms of understanding are interpretations, while others have taken the opposite camp by holding that all interpretations are based on a particular frame of understanding. However, there seems to be a general consensus in contemporary thinking that the two are so closely related that you cannot have one without the other. For some school of thought, it is this metaphysical search for the foundation of knowledge that is methodologically hermeneutical. For others who dislike the word metaphysics, this hermeneutical endeavor is basically an epistemological problem. Hermeneutics therefore seems to be the common grounds where the distinction between metaphysics and epistemology is reconciled. Whether it is viewed as a metaphysical enterprise or as an epistemological endeavor, what must be said here is that, it is this mental journey from interpretation to understanding and from understanding to interpretation that is the hermeneutic endeavor in contemporary search for meaning or certain knowledge.

Since Schleiermacher and Dilthey the term hermeneutics has assumed a wider understanding and has come to be used more and more frequently by representatives of the social and human sciences. For some it designates a movement in twentieth century philosophy (represented by Martin Heidegger, Hans-Georg Gadamer) or theology (represented by Bultmann and the New Hermeneutics). In literary studies, it is seen as a special method of interpreting literary texts.

For example, Wilhelm von Humboldt adopted the hermeneutic principles to the study of language and history. Johann Gustav Droysen limited its application to the examination of historical method and modes of interpretation of historical facts. Philip August Boeck developed linguistic studies which came to be known as philological hermeneutics. Edmund Husserl combined phenomenology and hermeneutics and developed a new way of philosophizing in his phenomenological theory of meaning and of meaning-Apprehension. In *Being and Time,* Heidegger gave a new meaning to the term hermeneutics by associating it with the whole enterprise of philosophizing. He saw the task of a philosopher as being hermeneutic. His investigation into the foundation of hermeneutic concepts, changed "the very character of traditional hermeneutics itself and disclosed new vistas for it, moving it away from traditional methodological concerns."*2* Thus in *Being and Time,* Heidegger developed a fundamental ontology for the disclosure of Being - *Dasein* through the hermeneutical manifestations. For him, the task of the manifestation of being is not only phenomenological as Husserl proposed, but is fundamentally hermeneutic. Heidegger's argument is that since "the methodological intent of phenomenological description is to interpret" and "the logos of the phenomenology of human existence has the character of *hermeneuein* _ (Greek - "to interpret")" interpretation, then phenomenology is basically hermeneutical. In Heidegger we see phenomenology and hermeneutics collapsing into a singular activity. He states this clearly in *Being and Time* when he wrote: "The phenomenology of Being-there is hermeneutic in the original sense of the word, because it signifies the business of interpretation."*3*

In the Heideggerian sense therefore, hermeneutics is seen as a tool for uncovering the ontological structure of Being. Following this Heideggerian hermeneutical reasoning, inculturation as a hermeneutical enterprise could be reasoned as a tool for uncovering the ontological structure of the divine - human relationship in the economy of salvation.

Hans-Georg Gadamer in his Book, *Truth and Method - Outline for_Philosophical Hermeneutics,* baptized and confirmed hermeneutics as a philosophical method by returning the new hermeneutical enterprise to its traditional grounds of the problem of interpretation and understanding. He ascribes primacy to the role of understanding. Unlike Schleiermacher, who conceived understanding as a means of overcoming what he described as "the historical distance" between the interpreter and "the historical phenomenon", Gadamer argues for the historical nature of understanding itself. For him:

> any interpretation of the past, whether they were performed by an historian, philosopher, linguist, or literary scholar, are as much a creature of the interpreter's own time and place as the phenomenon under investigation was of its own period of history.*4*

Thus for Gadamer, the interpreter is always guided in his understanding of the past by his own particular set of "prejudices" (Vor-urteil). Another position reached by Gadamer is that understanding is possible only if the object to be understood and the person involved in the act of understanding are not alien entities that are isolated from each other by a gulf of historical time. But, they initially stand in a state of relatedness to each other.

Following this Gadamerian hermeneutics of understanding, we can similarly talk about the historicity of inculturation in evangelization. Such discourse becomes very meaningful when we know that incarnation is related to creation as evangelization is related to incarnation. And what is more, that both the evangelizer and the evangelized are related initially by creation (in the image and likeness of God) and incarnation event. Creation, incarnation and evangelization can thus be reasoned as historical moments made manifest through inculturation. It must be noted here that the historical moments in question are not isolated moments but moments that are always related and understood in the light of the original moment.

6.2   Hermeneutics as the Foil for Understanding Inculturation.

The perception of incarnation as a form of inculturation and inculturation as incarnation; incarnation as evangelization and evangelization as a manifestation of incarnation; and inculturation as evangelization and evangelization as a type of inculturation, has introduced new dimensions of the divine - human relationship which can only be understood and appreciated within the matrix of a hermeneutical return. Inculturation is thus reasoned here as a hermeneutic activity. Hermeneutics is understood here, not only in the usual way of following its historical genesis from Schleiermacher and Dilthey, but also in a more radical understanding of the Heideggerian, Gadamerian and Derrida-ian traditions. In these traditions, hermeneutics is understood as a tool for uncovering the ontological structure of being and its varied manifestations.

The central contribution of all the scholars of hermeneutics lies in their claim that in any process of understanding, the parts, must be understood in relation to the whole, just as the whole can only be understood in relation to its parts. Following this hermeneutical reasoning, one can also say that incarnation can be best understood through the subsequent and various manifestations such as inculturation and evangelization. In the same vein, these manifestations can be properly understood if their interpretations are rooted in the original incarnation event.

John Paul II in his new method of evangelization sees inculturation as a return to the old and original tradition of evangelization. Because this return entails a new understanding and application in a much more dynamic way there is a sense of rupture and continuity. This makes the whole enterprise hermeneutical. But, apart from this historical return, there is, in John Paul II's thought a more fundamental hermeneutical dialogue that is involved in understanding the relationship between incarnation, inculturation and evangelization.

In the study of the history of the emergence of inculturation as an evangelization process, the closest attempt to relate hermeneutics to the process of inculturation is the work of Peter Schineller.5 Schineller   first stumbled into the hermeneutical cycle of inculturation when he attempted to evolve a relationship between what he described as the three poles of inculturation process, namely:

1) the situation,
2) the Christian message,
3) the pastoral agent or minister.6

He represented the inculturation hermeneutical cycle diagrammatically as:

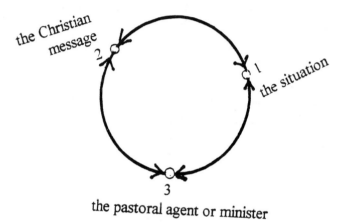

Fig. 1 Peter Schineller's model

Schineller presents this diagram as a demonstration of how inculturation works. The diagram he admits is difficult to understand.7 But he also admits that despite the difficulty, it is important for the understanding of how inculturation works. For him, the first example of a situation where inculturation is needed would be that of the missionary (evangelizer). This missionary could be:

> The priest in the rectory preparing his sermon ... a bishop or group of bishops writing a pastoral letter to their dioceses on justice or the evils of racism, a director of religious education beginning an assignment in a parish where a number of minority groups are represented, a lay person advising a friend or relative on choosing a career or vocation, a theologian writing an essay on the meaning of Sunday worship for the Christian community, a retreat director guiding a person through a weekend or five day retreat and finally a pastoral assistant (religious or lay) in a parish trying to reconcile a husband and wife after a prolonged and heated argument.*8*

These situations he admits vary with respect to both the identity of the ministers and the particular location they are confronted with. However, no matter how varied, Schineller thinks that every pastoral situation could be represented by the three pole relationship: the situation, the Christian message, the pastoral agent.

Schineller seems to lay the emphasis on the pastoral agent inculturating his Christian message within the context of the situation where evangelization is effected. This seems to imply a lapse into the old method of adaptation. For example, the bishop or group of bishops writing their pastoral letter must adapt their message to the felt pastoral needs and problems like justice or evils of racism. Similarly, all pastoral agents be they pastors, directors of religious education, theologians, etc., must inculturate their message to make it relevant to the context. Still, what inculturation means here for Schineller is unclear.

However, despite this unclarity, we must admit that Schineller has made a useful contribution by relating inculturation to hermeneutics. The only problem is that his analysis as it stands is incapable of explaining the internal dynamics of how inculturation actually works. For example, in explaining the relationship between the poles, he says, that the arrows between the poles indicate, that movement around the circle must proceed in both clockwise and counter clockwise directions. Why the movement must be both clockwise and counter clockwise at the same time, he does not say. Besides, the identification of the situation, Christian message and pastoral agent only points or indicates the pastoral environment without showing how they are related. An analogous example would be that of an observer who identifies the players in a soccer team without being able to explain how soccer is played. But, as already noted, Schineller in his attempt, has made a useful contribution. His reference to the relationship between the pastoral agent, the situation and the Christian message as being hermeneutical is insightful.

Our task here is to go further and propose the hermeneutical foil as the matrix for understanding the dynamics of inculturation, and inculturation itself will be examined as a hermeneutic method. In this process we would have succeeded in showing how inculturation actually works.

From the discussions in the previous chapters on Incarnation and Evangelization as processes of inculturation, it had become clear that incarnation, inculturation and evangelization are so interwoven that the mention of one necessarily entails the other.

Following the Schineller diagram, the poles can be substituted by the different inculturational modes in a way that brings out the hermeneutical relationships.

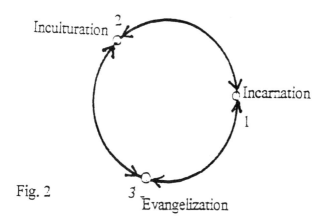

Fig. 2

The hermeneutical cycle of inculturation as it stands in the above diagram is loaded and complex. It can be further simplified to bring out six such circles of interwoven and interrelated relationships. Each representing a process of always returning to the original origin. The new original origin always being in a dynamic mode of continuous innermost direction and momentum of incarnating - inculturating - and evangelizing, each always serving as the starting point and as the end result.

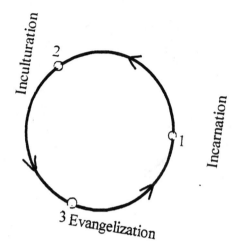

Fig. 3

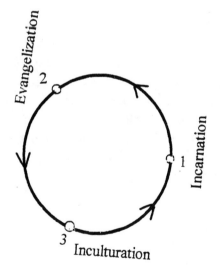

Fig. 4

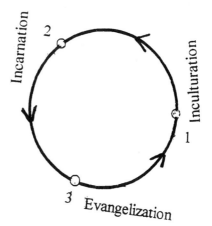

Fig. 5

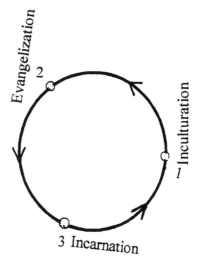

Fig. 6

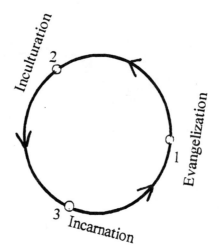

Fig. 7

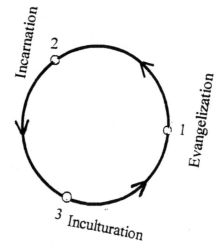

Fig. 8

The above diagrams (Fig.3-8) are examples of how the relationships are effected. In Fig.3, Incarnation is taken as the starting point. This incarnation process results in inculturation, and from inculturation it leads to evangelization. By God becoming man (incarnation), inculturation had taken place and this emergence of the divine in a human nature resulted in the evangelization of the human nature and culture. Such evangelization necessarily set in motion the process for the restoration of all things to God through Christ.

In Fig.8, the process begins with evangelization, leading to the incarnation of the word of God (goodnews) and the incarnation of the goodnews leads to the emergence or the perceiving of a new cultural form (inculturation) from within the existing culture that is being evangelized.

These two examples serve to illustrate how the process is effected in each of the moments of either incarnation or inculturation or evangelization.

The relationship can further be represented diagrammatically as follows:

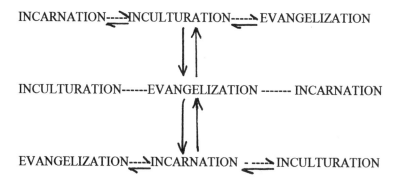

INCARNATION----→INCULTURATION----→EVANGELIZATION

INCULTURATION------EVANGELIZATION ------- INCARNATION

EVANGELIZATION---→INCARNATION ----→ INCULTURATION

Taking incarnation as the primal inculturation, inculturation today becomes a repeat which pushes forward and produces what it repeats, namely incarnation. Similarly, taking incarnation as a primal evangelization, evangelization today becomes a repeat of the original act - whose act it pushes forward and produces what it repeats, namely incarnation. Jesus said "just as the Father sent me, so also have I sent you". Here Jesus repeats the Fathers act. By repeating the *sending* of the Father, Jesus externalizes the original act. This is exactly what evangelization today means. A repeat of the original incarnational evangelism. In the same vein, inculturation as a form of evangelization is a repeat of the original inculturation which took place at the first incarnation.

This hermeneutical repetition is not a crude repetition but a repetition which produces something new. Thus we see that in the incarnation ⇇---> inculturation ⇇---> evangelization relationship, there is interwovenness and creativity. This is why Pope John Paul II, even though he knows that what he calls for is a return to the ancient tradition, yet he describes it as new evangelization. What is being repeated is not the old as old, but the old as new.

It is within this matrix of continuous incarnation and continuous evangelization that inculturation can be understood. And we can also say that it is within the conceptual frame of inculturation that incarnation and evangelization can become missiologically significant. Or to put it differently, we can say that it is inculturation that allows for the possibility of incarnation and evangelization. With this understanding, we can, therefore, see why Pope John Paul II has insisted so emphatically that inculturation must be the matrix of the new evangelization.

References

Chapter 6

1. Frederic Nietzsche, *On the Genealogy of Morals*, (New York: Vintage Books, 1969), p.80.

2. Kurt Mueller-Vollmer, *The Hermeneutics Reader*, (New York: Continuum Publishing Co., 1994), p.33.

3. Quotation cited in *The Hermeneutics Reader*, p.34.

4. Ibid., p.38.

5. Schineller, *A Hand Book on Inculturation* p. 61-71.

6. Ibid., p.62.

7. Ibid.

8. Ibid., 61.

CHAPTER 7

INCULTURATION AND THE LOGIC OF IDENTITY AND UNIVERSALITY

In most of Pope John Paul II's encyclicals and teachings, one of the most central theme is that of Christ who is the redeemer of the world and who penetrates in a unique unrepeatable way into the mystery of man and entered his heart. In fact he even adds that Christ is at the center of all human history and culture.*1* This definitely brings to mind the notion of the universality of Christianity and salvation offered by Christ. But how is this universality, unity and commonness to be explained in the face of the many diversities that exist in human cultures.

The purpose of this chapter is to attempt to explain the logic of the universality of the salvation brought by Christ through the incarnation event. We shall seek to do this with the use of the Venn Diagram. In the process, the question of the identity of cultures in the face of this universality will be addressed.

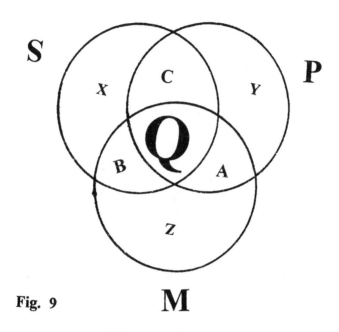

Fig. 9   **M**

Christ (represented by the letter Q in the diagram) is the universal element in all cultures and the center of the universe. By the fact of incarnation, all elements in all cultures have been transformed and christified. Not to accept this fact, is to limit the power and goal of the incarnation event, and a refusal to accept the universality of Christ. Christ confirmed his universal mission when he said: "I came that all may have life and have it more abundantly"(Jn.10:10).

In the diagram we have cultural universes or nations represented by M, S and P. By the fact of incarnation these cultural universes have become unified in Christ Q.

In the universe of M, M possesses z as a distinctive characteristic not shared by the others (S, P). In the universe of S, S possesses x as a distinctive characteristic not shared by others (M, P). In the universe of P, P possesses y as a distinctive characteristic not shared by others (S, M). It is these unshared characteristics (z, x, y) which give the distinctive identity of the different universes or cultures. But between S and M, they share B in common which allows for the possibility of S being similar to M. The same is also true of the relationship between S and P where they share C in common; and M and P where they share A in common. But between M, S, P, Q is the common element. By virtue of incarnation, all the cultures of S, P, and M have been affected.

Let M be the evangelizer to S. M must be able to recognize x, B, C and Q as elements in S that have been touched and affected by Christ represented by Q. Most of the time, because M himself has been touched by Christ, he is able to recognize the element B and Q which he shares in common with S as being Christian. In relation to B and Q then, M and S are Christian brothers brothers and sisters. The real problem of evangelization is in the capacity of M to see something good in x (of S) which is totally other. This is the crux of Christ's teaching when he said "if you love only those who love you, how are you different from the pharisees who look out only for their own" (Mt.5:43-48). Being able to see Christ in x (of S) is what it means to love the enemy, to go the extra mile, and to love the neighbor.

If real evangelization is to take place, M must be able to recognize the Christian element in x (of S) which is the distinctive character of S just as z is the distinctive character of M and have all been affected by the incarnation event. As St. Paul says, "in Christ all things have been sanctified and all is pure for those who are pure." What has been said here of the evangelization mission of M is also true of the evangelization mission of S and P.

It is for the respect of cultures and values that are characterized by x, y, and z, the unique characteristics that Pope John Paul II called for, when he said to the African bishops: "By respecting, preserving and fostering the particular values and riches of your peoples heritage, you will be in a position to lead them to a better understanding of the mystery of Christ."2

The operative expression in this quote is "the particular values and riches of peoples heritage." The reference here is not to the universal Christ-like values which are found in all cultures as represented by Q (or by B in M and S relationship or by A in M and P relationship or by C in S and P relatioship)in the diagram (Fig.9) rather, the Pope is referring specifically to those values that the incarnation event had transformed and are unique in each culture as represented by x, y, and z in the diagram. We must note that if there were no x, y, and z there would be no independent identities and distinctions. And if there were no distinctions and plurality, the sense of universality would be impossible. Difference and plurality are necessary for universality.

The likely objection that could be raised here is, if Christ has redeemed all cultures and Christ is to be found in all cultures, how then do the evangelizers eliminate those elements that are unchristian in cultures that they behold? The answer is simple and straight forward. Christ became like us in all things but sin. As he himself did with the Jewish culture, he identified with all things in the Jewish culture except those things that were offensive to God and human progress. As we learn in the history of the decalogue, whatever negates the wellbeing of the human person, who de facto and de jure (divine law) are created in the image and likeness of God, is offensive to God. It is in the light of this that such practices as killing of twins in some cultures and racism and murder by abortion are condemned as evil practices. It is imperative that the evangelizer, like Christ, must reject in any culture those things that are anti-God and anti-human progress. But the problem here is that the evangelizer must be careful not to put into the other's culture what does not belong to it in the name of trying to make them Christian. All of what Christ made of what was to become Christianity were of the Jewish culture. His task, as he said, was to purify, perfect and fulfill what was already there and not to destroy (Matt.5:17-19).On hindsight, this seems to have been the greatest problem of most post-apostolic evangelizers till today. They seek not to perfect but to destroy. This explains why Christian evangelism when not properly ordered is often associated with colonialism and imperialism.

This process of purifying culture includes the rejection of that which is antithetic and negative to human development but not a "putting in of" what is foreign to the culture. An example could be seen in Pope John Paul II's evangelical mission to the American Church. He told the American Church that they must resist the "culture of death" in the American society. Since life is a divine gift and an ontological mandate, anything that destroys human life whether directly or indirectly is tantamount to self negation and destruction. Such an act is against the will of God and against the essence of being, even for those who purport not to belief in God. On this ground, the Pope sees the legalization of abortion as evil. Here, while the Pope draws attention to what it is to be human, he does not in any way introduce anything that is foreign to the American culture. He is only asking man to return to his roots of self preservation as a human being.

In the evangelization mission, any attempt by M to

impose z (which he considers Christian in his own context) on
S is nothing but a cultural imposition precisely because S has
no room for z just as M itself has no room for x or y. A similar
logic of relationship exists between S and P and vice versa,
and P and M and vice versa. Bernard Lonergan had shared this
insight when he cautioned:

> In so far as one preaches the gospel as it has been developed
> with one's own culture, one is preaching not only the gospel
> but also one's own culture. In so far as one is preaching one's
> own culture, one is asking others not only to accept the gospel
> but also to renounce their own culture and accept one's own.[3]

What this new insight calls for is not the abandonment
of evangelization, but a new understanding that B and Q in the
diagram in Fig 9 serve as the bases of communality between
S and M. A and Q serve as the bases of communality between
M and P. C and Q serve as the bases of communality between
S and P. But Q which is the universal element serves as the
basis of universality. What is more, the more x, y, z are
recognized as having been affected by incarnation, and
therefore capable of leading people to Christ, the more
universal the Church of Christ becomes.

This kind of understanding of the logic of the necessity
of identity and the logic of the necessity of universality and
how they are related definitely highlights the need for
tolerance and reciprocal acceptance of the different cultural
personalities. The respect for differences and identification
with the common and universal elements would foster
communality and communion within both the particular and
the universal church. Instead of the usual search for unity in
diversity, with this new understanding of the logic of relations,
we would be working toward the achievement of diversity in
unity. Our starting point must unity and not diversity.

Diversity is centrifugally focused whereas unity is centripetal in nature.

As Eugene Hillman has argued:

> the incarnation of the divine word in Jesus of Nazareth necessarily entails the full acceptance of an historically conditioned culture, because, no human being exists outside a specific historically conditioned culture. In becoming Christians therefore, far from stepping out of their real-life situations, the peoples of the world are expected to be fully themselves in their respective historical contexts, and to enrich the universal Christian community with their particular cultural patrimonies.*4*

It is only after the kind of identification with all cultures that Christ initiated has been achieved then would we be able to redeem all things in Christ. It is also only after this has been done that Christ will come again to restore all things to the Father. Unless this is achieved the Second coming of Christ is still yet to come.

Pope John Paul II's theory of the logic of identity and universality has implications also in political and social relations. He carried his grammar to the theater of world politics during his address to the United Nations Assembly in New York (October 5, 1995). He noted the fact that despite the apparent end of the cold war, that the international community was still experiencing tension. He pointed to the fact that the world is still ravaged by violent ethnic and religious conflicts, with large segments of Third World nations facing economic and social crisis engineered partly by the engine of capitalism which imposes a form of economic triage that promotes rich for the few and poverty for the many. The reason for this unfortunate situation the Pope says is because "the world has yet to learn how to live with diversity." This situation according to the Pope could be remedied if peoples and nations will learn to tolerate differences in others and work together for a common good. The fact of "difference," and the reality of "the other," should not be seen as a threat but as a source of cooperation.

The Pope insisted that the freedom of the children of God is something that is universally cherished by all in all cultures. Therefore, since "this phenomenon is not limited to any one part of the world, nor is it expressed of any single culture,"5 the dignity of individuals, cultures and nations must be respected at all times. The United Nations Organization the Pope says:

> needs to rise more and more above the cold status of an administrative institution and become a moral center where all nations of the world feel at home and develop a shared awareness of being, as it were, a family of nations.6

Here we can see the consistency of the Pope's thought. The individual and varied cultures are uniquely important for perceiving and understanding reality as they are, for the progress of human society. They are to be encouraged for effective cooperation and mutual enrichment. The new political order should therefore have for its maxim: Diversity in Unity.

References

Chapter 7

1. *Redemptor Hominis*, no.1

2. Pope John Paul II, Address to the Representatives of the Cultural World, Yaounde, Cameroon, August 13, 1985.

3. Bernard Lonergan, *Method in Theology*, (New York: Herder and Herder, 1972), 99.362-363.

4. Eugene Hillman, *Toward an African Christianity: Inculturation Applied*, (New York: Paulist Press, 1993). P 2

5. PopeJohn Paul II,Address to the United Nation Assembly on the Occasion of the 50th Anniversary, NewYork,October 5, 1995.

6. Ibid.

CHAPTER 8

CONCLUSION

Pope John Paul II has been the author and great proponent of the new method and process of evangelization called inculturation. The concept takes into consideration the whole history of salvation beginning with creation and incarnation to the present day evangelization mission. It is rooted in the missiological character of God's salvific activity. The concept which has been defined universally as both an act and a process by which a new cultural form emanates from or is perceived in an already existing one has broken new grounds and has effected an epistemological shift in the perception and understanding of evangelization.

The text began in Chapter One with a search for a definition of inculturation. Then, Chapter Two, proceeded to investigate the development of the term and its evolution in the thought of John Paul II.

Chapter Three focused on inculturation and evangelization with specific attention to themes such as creation as inculturation, incarnation as inculturation and evangelization as inculturation.

Chapter Four dealt with what Pope John Paul II says specifically about the new method of evangelization. In Chapter Five, the person and actions of Pope John Paul II were examined as symbols of inculturation

Chapter Six focused on the relationship between hermeneutics and inculturation and argued that hermeneutics is the most rational foil for understanding the mechanics and logic of inculturation. Then Chapter Seven which is rather short because of its diagramatic nature tried to trace the logic of identity and universality within the inculturation framework.

Creation the text has argued is God extending His being in otherness. By creating, He brings to being the human nature. A mixing of the divine nature with the creaturely nature. This, the text sees as a type of inculturation.

With the debasement of the human nature through sin, God did not abandon man. He still wanted to redeem man. He sent his son to assume the human nature so as to reclaim it for Himself. This incarnation event is seen as a type of inculturation.

Incarnation is God entering into the human nature. The divine culture enters into the human nature, assumes it and makes it whole again. Christ did not change the human nature but assumed it as it was and is. Thus restoring man to his original state. This restoration of the debased human nature to its original state through Christ is a type of inculturation.

The text sees the sending of the son as an evangelization mission to mankind. Jesus Christ himself sends the Church to continue to bring the goodnews to the ends of the earth. The Holy Spirit which is sent by the Father together with the Son is the active agent of the church's evangelizing mission.

Evangelization is defined in the text as the proclamation of God's salvation to the ends of the earth. But since this had already been achieved by Christ through incarnation, the mission of evangelization today is to go out and proclaim and witness to the presence of Christ in the world. This type of evangelization by recognizing and proclaiming what is already there is a form of inculturation especially as it brings out a new way of perceiving reality that is already there but hidden. It was within the context of this type of evangelization that Pope John Paul II defined inculturation as the incarnation of the gospel (goodnews)in autochthonous cultures, at the same time the introduction of those cultures into the life of the Church. This definition the text argues, highlights the notion of reciprocity in the evangelization process.

The process by which God enters into human history whether through creation or incarnation is what is conceived in the text as divine inculturation. The act and the process by which the presence of Christ is witnessed as present in human cultures is what is understood as human inculturation in today's evangelization mission. But, both the divine and human inculturation in the evangelization process are so interwovenly related that the one cannot do without the other.

The paradigm of perception that has evolved with the concept of inculturation as discussed in the text, definitely has a wider implication in other fields of endeavor, especially philosophy, social and human sciences. Apart from providing theologians and missiologists with a paradigm for understanding the notion of evangelization, philosophically, it serves as a unifying principle that would usher in a new world order (intellectually and socially), wherein diversity of culture will be an instrument not of division but cooperation and unity. Pope John Paul II said it all on October 5, 1995, when he addressed the United Nations Assembly in these words:

If we make the effort to look at matters objectively, we can see that, transcending all the differences which distinguish individuals and peoples, there is a fundamental communality. For different cultures are but different ways of facing the question of the meaning of personal existence ... Every culture is an effort to ponder the mystery of the world and in particular of the human person. It is a way of giving expression to the transcendent dimension of human life ... Our respect for the culture of others is therefore rooted in our respect for each community's attempt to answer the question of human life. *1*

With this new paradigm of perception, philosophical endeavors will no longer be viewed as activities whose task is aimed at cultural imperialism but engagements whose aim is to discover the various manifestations of reality as are embedded in the varied cultures. Political strategies will no longer be designed for the purpose of impoverishing other nations but aimed at achieving a world community with mutual needs and aspirations. A world community where cooperation and not domination will be a priority. This definitely would lead to a more peaceful world where human dignity is respected and the autonomy of nations cherished.

Thus, through inculturation as a theoretical mind set, Christianity and democracy will each, become not a formula but a destiny, not an idealogy but a task, not a utopia but a direction which enables us to see in others what we see in ourselves, and see in ourselves what we see in others. It is only when this has been achieved that the true Christian community and world community would have been built through out the ends of the earth.

Pope John Paul II has been the author and great proponent of this new method and process of evangelization and world view. He is thus and justifiably the Father of Inculturation.

Reference

Chapter 8

1. Pope John Paul II, Address to the United Nations Assembly on the Occasion of the 50th Anniversary, New York, October 5, 1995.

BIBLIOGRAPHY

Primary Sources

Pope John Paul II, Encyclical, *Ut Unum   Sint* (That They May Be
    One), May 5, 1995.
----, Encyclical, *Evangelium Vitae* (The Gospel of Life), March 25,
    1995
----, *Crossing the Threshold of Hope*, (New York:Alfred   Knopf
    1994).
----, Encyclical, *Veritatis Splendor* (The Splendor of the Truth), August
    6, 1993.
----, Encyclical, *Centesimus Annus* (The Hundredth Year),   May 1,
    1991.
----, Encyclical, *Redemptoris Missio* (The Mission of the
    Redeemer), December 7, 1990.
----, Encyclical, *Sollicitudo Rei Socialis* (Solicitude for   Social
    Matters), December 30, 1987.
----, Encyclical, *Redemptoris Mater* (The Mother of the Redeemer),
    March 25, 1987.
----, *Address to the Pontifical Council for Culture*, January 7, 1978.
----, Encyclical, *Dominum et Vivificantem* (Lord and Giver of Life),
    May 18, 1986.
----, Encyclical, *Slavorum Apostoli* (Apostles of the Slavonic People),
    June 2, 1985.
----, *Address to the Extra-Ordinary Synod of Bishops*, 1985.
----, *Address to the Latin American Bishops*, 1983.
----, Apostolic Exhortation, *Familiaris Consortio*, 1981.

----, Encyclical, *Laborem Exercens* (On Human Work), September 14, 1981.

----, *Address to African Bishops,* Kenya, 1980.

----, "Man's Humanity Is Expressed in Culture", *Address to* UNESCO,   June 2, 1980.

----, Encyclical, *Dives in Misericordia* (On the Mercy of God), November 30, 1980.

----, Apostolic Exhortation, *Catechesi Tradendae*, October 16, 1979.

----, Encyclical, *Redemptor Hominis* (Redeemer of Man), March 4, 1979.

Wojtyla, K.(Pope John Paul II), *Love and Resposibility*, Translated by H.T. Willetts, (New York: Farrar, Straus and Giroux, 1981).

----, *Sources of Renewal: The Implementation of Vatican II*, Translated by P. S. Falla, (New York: Harper & Row, 1980).

----, *The Acting Person*, Edited by Anna - Teresa Tymieniecka, Translated by Andrzej Potocki, Vol. 10: *Analecta Husserliana*, The Year Book of Phenomenological Research, (Dordrecht, Holland: D. Reidel Publishing Co., 1979.)

Other Sources

Arrupe, P., "Letter to the Whole Society on Inculturation",*International Apostolate of Jesuits*, 2,7, 13.

Avery, D., *The Reshaping of Catholicism,* (New York: Harper and Row, 1988).

Biffi, G., et al (ed.), *John Paul II: A Panorama of His Teaching* (New York: New City Press, 1989).

Blomjours, J., "Inculturation and Interculturation" *AFER* 22, 1980, pp.393-398.

Conger, Y., *Diversity and Communion*, (Connecticut: Twenty-Third Publication, 1985).

Crollius, A.A.R., *Inculturation*, (Rome: Gregorian University Press , 1987).

Donovan, V.J., *Christianity Rediscovered*, (New York: Orbis Books, 1983).

Frossard, A., *Portrait of John Paul II*, (San Francisco: Ignatius Press, 1990).

--------------- and Pope John Paul II, *Be Not Afraid*, (New York: St. Martin's Press,1984).

Gremillion, J., *The Church and Culture since Vatican II*, (Indiana: University of Notre Dame Press, 1985).

Gutierrez, G., *We Drink from Our Own Wells*, (New York: Orbis Books, 1985).

Hacker, P., *Theological Foundations of Evangelization*, (Koln, Steyler Verlag, 1993).

Hillman, E., *Inculturation Applied: Toward an African Christianity*, (New York: Paulist Press, 1993).

Hogan, R.M., and LeVoir, J.M., *Covenant of Love: Pope John Paul II on Sexuality, Marriage, and Family in the Modern World*, (San Francisco: Ignatius Press, 1992).

Bernard Lonergan, *Method in Theology*, (New York: Herder and Herder, 1972).

Mccormack, A., *The Third World - The Teaching of Pope John Paul II*, (London: C.T.S., 1982).

Niebuhr, H. r., *Christ and Culture*, (New York: Harper and row, 1951).

Mueller-Vollmer, K., (ed.), *The Hermeneutics Reader*, (New York: Continuum Publishing Co., 1994).

Nemec, L., *Pope John Paul II: A Festive Profile* (New York: Catholic Book Publishing, 1979) chs.8,10,15.

Okure, T. "Inculturation in the New Testament: Its Relevance for the Nigerian Church", *Inculturation In Nigeria*,(Lagos: CSN Publication, 1989).

Onwubiko, O.A., *Theory and Practice of Inculturation*, (Enugu: SNAAP Press, 1992).

Ralph, M., and Peter, W., *John Paul II and the New Evangelization*, (San Francisco: Ignatius Press, 1995).

Rooney, J., The Changing Faces of Mission, (London: C.T.S.,1983).

Rynne, X., *John Paul's Extraordinary Synod*, (Wilmingtonz: Michael Glazier, 1986).

Sarpong, P.K., "Inculturation and African Church" *Shalom* 6, 1988, pp.76-87.

Schineller, P., *A Hand Book on Inculturation*, (New York: Paulist Press, 1990).

Schreiter, r., *Constructing Local Theologies*, (New York: Orbis Books,

1985)
Shorter, A., *Towards an African Theology of Inculturation*
(New York Orbis Books, 1988).
Seifert, J., "Karol Cardinal Wojtyla (Pope John Paul II) as Philosopher
and the Cracow/Lublin School of Philosophy." *Aletheia* Vol.2, (1981),
pp.130-199.
Ukpong, J., "Towards a Renewed Approach to Inculturation
Theology", *Journal of Inculturation*, Vol.1, 1994, pp.8-24.
---, (ed.), *Evangelization in Africa in the Third Millenium*, (Port
Harcourt: CIWA Press, 1992).
Wallingo, J.M., (ed.) *Inculturation: Its Meaning and Urgency*, (Nairobi,
Kenya: St. Paul Publications, 1986).

Other Documents.

Vatican II Documents.

Pope Paul VI, *Ecclesiam Suam*, AAS, 56(1964) 10
----, *Evangelii Nuntiandi*, AAS, 68(1976)5.
The Extraordinary Synod, 1985.
The Lineamenta, Synod of Bishops: Special Assembly for Africa and
Her Evangelizing Mission Towards the Year 2000, "You Shall *be My
Witness*" (Acts 1:18), Vatican City, 1990.
Inculturation in Nigeria, Proceedings of Nigerian Catholic Bishops
Study Session, November 1988.
The Nigerian Church: Evangelization through Inculturation,
Pastoral Letter by the Catholic Bishops Conference of Nigeria, 1991.

INDEX

About the Author

December 15, 1951 ---- Born of the family of Mr. and Mrs. Alexis Obot Udoidem in Ikot Abasi Akpan, Akwa Ibom State, Nigeria
1955 - 1963 ----- Pre-primary and Primary School at St. Christopher's School, Ikot Abasi Akpan and Christ the King School, Uyo. Graduated with a First School Certificate.

1964 - 1970----- Preparatory Seminary and Secondary Education at Regina Caeli Secondary School and Queen of Apostle's Seminary. Graduated with a London General Certificate of Education (G.C.E.).

1971 - 1977 ---- Admitted in Saints Peter and Paul Major Seminary, Ibadan, for Graduate Studies in Philosophy and Theology and allied Sciences. Graduated with a Diploma (Distinction)in Religious Studies from the University of Ibadan, (1975). Appointed Music Master in the Seminary (1975 - 77). Earned a Bachelors degree in Philosophy and Theology (1977).

December 10, 1977 ---- Ordained Priest for the Diocese of Calabar (Now Archdiocese) by His Eminence Dominic Cardinal Ekanem (late) at the Sacred Heart Cathedral.

1978 - 1979 ---- Appointed Principal and Tutor, Assumption Girls Juniorate, Uyo, by His Grace, Most Rev. Brian D. Usanga, D.D., (then bishop of Calabar) , Archbishop of Calabar Metropolitan See. Served as the Pastor of Assumption Parish, Ndon Ebom and St. John's Parish, Okobo.

1980 - 1981 ---- -Appointed Tutor, Immaculate Conception Seminary, Calabar. Served as Pastor of St. Michael, Oban, and St. John, Asong.

September 1981- 1985 ---- Admitted for Advanced studies at the graduate School of Philosophy, Catholic University of America, Washington, D.C.; Earned a Masters Degree in Philosphy of Science with a Thesis, *Isaac Newton on the Concept of 'Impressed Force' in the Principia;* (1983), and a Doctorate degree in Social and Political Philosophy (Ph.D) with a dissertation, *Authority and the Common Good in the Social and Political Philosophy of Yves R. Simon, (December10,*

1985.

1982 - 1985 ---- Served as the Associate Pastor at St. Francis de Sales Church, Kilmarnock in the diocese of Arlington, Virginia; and Resident Chaplain for the Holy Cross Brothers, csc, Washington, D.C.; Founding President, African Student Association, Catholic University of America (1983-85).

1985 - 1986 ---- Assistant Professor of Philosophy, Howard University, Washington, D.C. Associate Pastor, St. Augustine Church, ashington, DC.

1987 - 1989 --- Returned to Nigeria as a Lecturer I at the University of Port Harcourt. Appointed Associate Chaplain of the Catholic Chaplaincy in the university. Published, *Authority and the Common Good in the Social and Political Philosophy*, University Press of America, Lanham, MD, 1988.

1990 - 1995--- Promoted Senior Lecturer and appointed Head of Philosophy Department, University of Port Harcourt; Appointed First Resident Catholic Chaplain, University of Port Harcourt; Appointed Chairman, Canon Law Commission, Diocese of Uyo. Appointed Member, University of Port Harcourt Senate. Published two books: *Understanding Philosophy*, (Lagos: African Heritage Publications, 1990) and *Values and National Development,* (Lagos: Afrocan Heritage Publications, 1992), over two dozens of Articles in Learned Journals and Books.

1995 - 1996 --- Visiting Research Professor, Council for Research in Values and Philosophy, Catholic University of America, Washington, DC. Appointed Parochial Vicar, St Andrew Catholic Church by Most Rev. David B. Thompson, Bishop of Charleston, U.S.A.

Fall 1996 --- Research Professor, Center for Philosophy of Religion, University of Notre Dame, Indiana. Associate Pastor, St. Hedwig Parish, South Bend, Indiana.

Current address (1996 - 97 session):
Rev. Fr. S. Iniobong Udoidem
Professor of Philosophy
Center for Philosophy of Religion
330 Decio Hall, P.O. Box 1068
University of Notre Dame
Notre Dame, Indiana 46556